INFLUENCE
FOR IMPACT

INFLUENCE
FOR IMPACT
INCREASING YOUR EFFECTIVENESS IN THE ORGANIZATION

Hodges L. Golson, Ph.D.

iUniverse, Inc.
New York Lincoln Shanghai

Influence for Impact
Increasing Your Effectiveness in the Organization

iUniverse books may be ordered through booksellers or by contacting:

iUniverse
2021 Pine Lake Road, Suite 100
Lincoln, NE 68512
www.iuniverse.com
1-800-Authors (1-800-288-4677)

A version of this text is available as a streaming video at
www.influenceforimpact.com

ISBN-13: 978-0-595-38166-1 (pbk)
ISBN-13: 978-0-595-83649-9 (cloth)
ISBN-13: 978-0-595-82533-2 (ebk)
ISBN-10: 0-595-38166-9 (pbk)
ISBN-10: 0-595-83649-6 (cloth)
ISBN-10: 0-595-82533-8 (ebk)

Printed in the United States of America

Contents

INTRODUCTION 1

What Do Successful People Look Like? 1

At the Most Basic Level, Peak Performance Depends on Four Foundation Competencies—the I-Competencies....*1*

Context: The Nature of Our Work...3

A Self-Assessment 4

CHAPTER 1   ORGANIZATIONAL CONTEXT:
                       HOW WORK GETS DONE....................................... 9

The Cycle of Results..9

The Goal: Primary Importance *9*

The Other Keys to Task Accomplishment *11*

Foundations of Credibility: Three More Keys to Success 11

The Task Dimension..*12*

The People Dimension *12*

Interaction Effects *13*

One Best Way?..*18*

Self-Management: The Integrating Dimension *19*

Summary...20

CHAPTER 2   A WIDELY SHARED OBSTACLE............................. 22

The Developmental Needs of Successful and High-Potential Leaders 22

Why Is This an Issue? 24

Why Are Influence Skills in Such Short Supply? 24

Influence and Personality...27

The Trait of Extraversion *29*

Emotional Intelligence...30

Summary...32

CHAPTER 3   THE FIRST FOUNDATIONS: CHARACTERISTICS OF THE EFFECTIVE PERSUADER..............................34

Credibility..34

The I-Competencies: Keys to Credibility...34

Other Considerations and Suggestions...36

The Law of Authority Is Essential to Establishing Credibility—
It Is Closely Associated with Expertise...36

The Law of Trust...38

The Law of Liking...40

Summary...44

CHAPTER 4   GENERAL LAWS OF INFLUENCE AND PERSUASION ..47

Remember What Motivates People...47

More Principles of Influence...48

The Law of Authority (Again)...48

The Law of Reciprocity...49

The Law of Consistency...50

The Law of Scarcity...52

The Law of Social Comparison...53

Summary...54

CHAPTER 5   MAKING YOUR CASE...56

Presentation Skills...56

Do Your Homework...56

Making the Pitch—Practical Tips...58

Summary...61

CHAPTER 6   SALES SCHOOL FOR NON-SALES TYPES: YOU NEED TO KNOW WHAT THEY KNOW!...........63

So What Can We Learn from Sales Training?...63

Other Applications of Sales Training Concepts: Focus on the Positive 66

The Negative (Pessimistic) Explanatory Style...67

The Positive (Optimistic) Explanatory Style...67

The ABC Model—Changing the Way You Think Changes the Way You Feel...67

Summary...69

CHAPTER 7   ORGANIZATIONAL SURVIVAL SKILLS AND
             PRACTICAL ADVICE 70
    Your Organizational Culture...70
    Starting Off on the Right Foot 71
    After the Transition 73
    Working on Teams 75
        The Characteristics of Effective Teams 75
        Team Roles.. 76
    Getting Feedback 77
    In Times of Stress 78
    Summary...80

CHAPTER 8   CONFLICT, CONFRONTATION,
             AND DIFFICULT INTERACTIONS 83
    Handling Conflict...84
    Assumptions and Consequences 86
    Guidelines for Handling Conflict.......................................87
    Summary...88

CLOSING SUGGESTIONS 91

APPENDIX 93
    Clusters of Developmental Needs..94
    Data from Executive Development Projects...........................96

REFERENCES 99

INDEX 103

INTRODUCTION

For this book, I draw on academic training and certification (Ph.D. in social psychology, licensure in Applied Psychology, and certification as an Industrial/ Organizational Psychologist by the American Board of Professional Psychology) as well as the practical experience I've gained by personally conducting over ten thousand psychological assessments in my career. I also draw on the experiences and insights of the smartest people I've ever met: my colleagues (who are also licensed psychologists) and my clients. These ideas and observations are also based on data from over fifty years of research in social psychology and other disciplines on influence, persuasion, and attitude change.

A training version of this book is available as a three-hour streaming video at www.influenceforimpact.com.

What Do Successful People Look Like?

Clients often ask, "What are the characteristics of high performers?" Success competencies are a function of the knowledge, skills, abilities, and personal characteristics that enable a person to perform well in a particular job. Although there are many different specific success profiles for different jobs, there are similarities in people who do well across jobs and companies.

There are two basic types of competencies. The *foundation* competencies are built into the system for the most part. These are the innate abilities and the enduring behavioral patterns we get through the luck of the draw from the gene pool and from our early learning and background experiences. This is the raw material we have to work with. The *surface* competencies are the result of later training and experience in schools, early jobs, and other learning experiences. People can develop a wide range of surface competencies depending on the types of foundation competencies they possess.

At the Most Basic Level, Peak Performance Depends on Four Foundation Competencies—the I-Competencies.

These competencies are described in greater depth in Chapter 3.

1

The Intellectual Competency. Some facets of this competency can be developed (e.g., by learning the use of various analysis and problem-solving techniques, by learning to reorient one's perspective more toward the global and strategic), but there are critical components here that are seemingly hardwired. Training and coaching in this area is usually not a good investment.

The Interpersonal Competency. The subset of this competency that we call "influence" is the focus of this book. This is the success factor that straddles the gap between the foundation and surface competencies. Although some of the facets that make up this competency are seemingly hardwired into the structure of personality, it is the one competency in this group that can be significantly developed with appropriate analysis, diagnosis, effort, and training.

The Integrity Competency. People can learn to be more consistent and to follow through with details and commitments more appropriately, but if they have a basic problem getting others to trust them, nothing else matters much. This is a very difficult area to change if the problem is rooted in basic values and personality structure rather than in naïveté or ignorance of appropriate norms and behavior.

The Intensity Competency. This is also a factor that is quite difficult to change. Our levels of stamina and energy can certainly improve with better health habits, but this performance factor also includes the basic drive and motivation toward accomplishment. Unfortunately, some people lack these basic characteristics, and there seems to be little we can do to make significant changes here over time if the problem lies in basic constitution or chronic passivity.

Our clear experience is that there is a process of selection (some of which is self-selection) that weeds out people with significant gaps in any of these four competencies. However, it is also our experience that there are many people who ascend to the middle executive or key individual performer ranks who have some spottiness in a variety of these dimensions. As the Appendix shows, the most frequent developmental need is in the influence/persuasion facet of the interpersonal competency. The bad news is that it takes a little effort to develop this set of skills. The good news is that they are developable, in contrast to some of the deficits associated with the other success competencies.

Context: The Nature of Our Work

As psychologists who work in the real world of business applications, we rely as much on observation and practical experience as on academic research to help our clients, but our practice is based on scientific research. Our primary reasons for being in business are to help our clients get the right people in the right jobs and to help people on the job meet their full potential. To do that, we employ all appropriate tools at our disposal. The most important and useful of these tools is the psychological assessment. It is a cornerstone of our work. The assessment consists of a structured interview that covers the person's background, educational and work experience, self-perceptions, insights, and general goals. It also includes standardized testing and personality inventories. Psychological assessment is a unique and valuable source of data, which can be used for the selection of and development of people. Although the effectiveness of the psychological assessment has been validated in many ways over a wide range of environments, the Appendix to this paper offers clear return-on-investment data further illustrating the usefulness of this tool.

The impetus for this book was the observation that many, if not most, successful executives have sometimes significant gaps in the soft skills of influence and insight. We come to these conclusions after many thousands of psychological assessments on high-level executives, developmental assessments for people in high-potential programs, and extensive experience coaching successful leaders.

The explicit assumption of this book is that you're interested in improving your ability to get what you want by gaining more power in the organization. We intend to help you do this by presenting what psychologists have learned about interpersonal skills, persuasion, and influence in a useful, practical format.

Some of the seminal insights about influence and persuasion generated by early academic studies are still very applicable.[1] Much of this research focused on questions of compliance and conformity and on finding ways to change attitudes and behavior. It sought to answer troubling questions about how seemingly normal people could make such bad decisions in response to authority (e.g., Nazi Germany). However, insights from social influence research have been used to help all sorts of people and organizations present their messages more effectively. Although this material is written primarily for people who need to increase their impact in their organizations by further developing and applying skills of influence and persuasion, these observations, research findings, and suggestions can be of benefit to anyone, even seasoned salespeople. They can help anyone who wants to increase his or her ability to understand, persuade, and influence others.

---

1   e.g., Milgram (1974), Zimbardo and Ebbesen (1970)

One of the keys to establishing credibility (a cornerstone of influence) is trust. If people don't trust you, you'll eventually have no ability to influence them, unless you're the boss. And if you're a boss people don't trust, you'll soon realize that they can be very clever in finding ways to help you fail. Therefore, we assume you realize that although the research, principles, and suggestions presented on the following pages can be used in a manipulative manner, it will only erode your effectiveness over time if you use them that way. Besides obvious ethical consider-ations, and from a purely pragmatic viewpoint, if you're perceived as manipulative or untrustworthy, you'll be toast in a short while.

A Self-Assessment

Before we know where we are going, we need to be sure we know where we are. As a first step to increasing your powers of influence, you need to know where your gaps and strengths are likely to be. To facilitate this process of insight development, please complete the following brief self-diagnostic instrument. As with all self-descriptive instruments, the accuracy of your results will depend on the accuracy of your self-perceptions and your willingness to answer in a straight-forward manner.

Read each statement and determine how much you think it describes your behavior on the job. Be honest with yourself or this is a waste of time. If you're unsure about some of the answers, get input from others who know you at work and who have had a chance to observe your behavior. The responses are:

   0 = Usually Not True

   1 = Sometimes True

   2 = Usually True

   3 = Always True

After scoring yourself on the items, record the total number of points for each factor in the spaces immediately below them. At the end, add all of the scores of the individual Factor Totals and record that figure in the Sum of All Factor Totals space.

Factor A

____ I find appropriate ways to make sure people know about my credentials and expertise. If I don't have expert credentials, I enlist the aid of those who do, or I find authoritative sources that agree with my position.

____ I pay attention to the image I project. I typically dress the part of the authority figure.

____ I actively try to be a good resource of accurate data and information. I show the logic, data, and reasoning behind my position to help people understand and accept it.

___ FACTOR A TOTAL

Factor T

____ I always follow through and meet my commitments.

____ I never exaggerate or oversell, and I acknowledge the validity of other points of view when they have merit.

____ I never betray confidences.

___ FACTOR T TOTAL

Factor L

____ I try to develop acquaintances and friends at work, finding shared interests and common ground.

____ I try to make people feel good and to show them that we're a lot alike.

____ I show an active interest in people and encourage them to talk about themselves.

___ FACTOR L TOTAL

Factor R

____ I do small favors for others whenever I have the chance.

____ I always try to do something helpful for the other person first.

____ I let others do me favors, even when I may not need them.

___ FACTOR R TOTAL

Factor C

___ I try to get others to agree with small requests before asking for a larger commitment.

___ I get others to state their opinions and/or to agree with my requests or ideas in public when possible.

___ I present my case in such a way that the other person will realize he's being consistent with his previous positions by agreeing with it.

___ FACTOR C TOTAL

Factor S

___ I show how my ideas or position will help the other person avoid some sort of loss.

___ I make sure others see that my information is new or in short supply and consequently that they need to make good use of it before it's widely known.

___ I appeal to their fear of losing something to help me persuade people to my point of view.

___ FACTOR S TOTAL

Factor SC

___ I try to find out as much as possible about the people and groups that are important to the other person before making my case.

___ I try to get active participation from others in the problem-solving and decision-making process.

___ I show how my solutions will be well accepted by the peer groups that are important to the other person.

___ FACTOR SC TOTAL

___ **SUM OF ALL FACTOR TOTALS (Find your sum in the ranges below.)**

0–21:   Finish this book ASAP!! Then read it again.

22–42:   Good. You're ahead of the game but need a little polish in some areas.

43–63:   Why aren't you out selling?

OK, so this isn't a rigorous statistical tool. However, it will help bring some things into focus for you and help in the self-diagnostic process as you read the following chapters. Keep your individual factor scores handy for later reference.

CHAPTER 1

Organizational Context: How Work Gets Done

Everything you do in an organization is about getting results. It's why organizations exist. The real measure of success in an organization is how well a person achieves results. To do so, one must be able to influence others. Even the most solitary individual contributors need to have influence so that their contributions will be accepted and therefore have an impact on results.

Power is a resource that can be used to change the behavior of others and to get results. Influence is the application of that resource. Power can come from your position in the organization (if you're the boss, your power comes from hierarchical authority). Power can also come from your own personal characteristics and behaviors (e.g., charisma or expertise).

You can gain influence by being able to solve problems cleverly, being able to recognize and explain good solutions developed by others, and being able to persuade others of the merit of your own solutions or ideas. You can also gain influence by being a good colleague or subordinate and by helping others to get their own needs met. If you do these things consistently over time, you will be seen as a resource for others, and therefore you will begin to be able to influence them more effectively. As your influence increases, your power to have a greater impact on the results of the organization increases.

As a prelude to the exploration of ways to increase your own influence and power within an organization, it will help to clearly understand how results are achieved. The Cycle of Results described below offers a conceptual framework for doing so.[1]

The Cycle of Results

The Goal: Primary Importance

Work is accomplished in a series of steps in a predictable cycle. Before anything can be accomplished, there must be a goal that provides the vision of the

---

1 Wilson (1985)

accomplishment. This is the absolute cornerstone of achieving results. Author, former business school dean, and corporate transformation expert Robert Miles notes that the clear and compelling goal is the first step in the implementation of transformational vision.[2] The importance of the goal can't be overemphasized. Many textbooks have been written and much research has been published on this topic. This is the first and most important step in the Cycle of Results. Its importance to influence is obvious—we need to know what we want the other to think or do before we can know the best way to get him or her to accept our ideas. The goal frames our efforts and channels them in the right direction.

But goals need to have certain characteristics to be effective. First, they must be clear. Everyone must understand them. If goals are fuzzy, the plans will be fuzzy, and therefore the results will be fuzzy. For instance, "Our goal is to be a world-class service provider" sounds nice, but how do you know it when you see it? What are the metrics and definitions? Or "I'm going to lose ten pounds." Sound familiar? This is a little better because it includes a measurable result. But it still doesn't offer enough definition about when or how this will be accomplished and consequently will probably end up in the dustbin of good intentions like so many other resolutions. Goal clarity gets everyone aligned and moving in the same direction.

Second, the goal must be perceived as worthwhile and important. People must feel that it is of value and worth their time to expend energy toward its accomplishment. "We're going to put a man on the moon by the end of the decade" was a very effective goal statement. The end result was clear; it provided a target that people felt was worthwhile and uplifting. It also provided the third component of the effective goal: a clear time frame.

If we don't know how long we have to accomplish something, it's too easy to procrastinate. People work better with deadlines. The best deadlines place just the right amount of pressure on the person or group without being unrealistic. We must know that the goal can be accomplished within the time frame, or we won't get fully engaged.

Implied by the idea of goal clarity is the need for clear, unambiguous measurement. Few goals will be as clear as President Kennedy's moon goal. Therefore, we need to be sure we have ways to know when we've accomplished the goal. What are the standards? How is it measured?

In summary, the goal is the most important step in achieving results.

---

2   Miles (1997)

The Other Keys to Task Accomplishment

Although the goal is of utmost importance in the Cycle of Results, there are other things that must happen after the goal is defined.

- **Planning.** After the goal has been established, we need to know how we're going to accomplish it. There must be a process of planning, resource gathering, and general problem anticipation/solving to allow us to move forward.

- **Facilitating.** This includes helping others to achieve results defined by the goal and plan. It involves facilitating, helping, coaching, coordinating, and doing whatever is necessary to remove obstacles for peers and subordinates. It may take the form of training, supporting, and instructing. This is central to teamwork.

- **Monitoring.** The adage "inspect what you expect" is applicable here. To ensure that the proper results are accomplished, one must be able to give and receive accurate feedback. There need to be effective lines of communication both ways.

- **Controlling.** Depending on the feedback from the monitoring process, adjustments may be needed along the way. When things are off-schedule or off-plan, changes need to be made. This is the essence of managing performance. It requires an active, not passive, approach.

- **Completing.** There are components of this phase of the cycle that are too easily and too often overlooked. There should be a process of closure that involves celebrating success and reinforcing good performance. There should also be an analysis of what went well and what should be improved upon next time. The attitude should be a positive and open "what can we learn?"

Foundations of Credibility: Three More Keys to Success

The importance of the goal cannot be stressed too strongly, and the previous discussion illustrates the process of getting results after the goal has been articulated. The goal is the first key to accomplishment, which is essential to credibility. The three other primary keys to success and credibility are task management, people management, and self-management. The task and people clusters have been referred to as autocratic vs. participative, assertive vs. democratic, forceful vs. enabling, etc. By whatever names, they have been a mainstay of research into leadership for over fifty years.[3] The following sections describe the Task, People,

---

3   Bass (1990)

and Self-Management Dimensions, which are crucial to gaining influence and achieving results.

The Task Dimension

The person who focuses most intensely on this dimension is typically described as results directed, task oriented, driving, and production focused. At least part of the production-orientation behavioral pattern is related to personality traits. Research and observation show that the most effective leaders and managers have reasonably high scores on personality factors associated with task orientation, provided they have the versatility to balance this aspect of their personality with sufficient concern for people. This is a necessary duality for successful leadership and organizational influence.[4]

Some of the more important skills related to this dimension are:

- Defining and structuring
- Communicating—sending/receiving feedback, providing critique
- Planning
- Monitoring
- Anticipating demands and problems
- Organizing
- Delegating
- Solving problems
- Maintaining control
- Setting subgoals
- Setting standards and making sure they are maintained

The Task Dimension cluster is often thought of as the "hard skills" and is obviously important in the Cycle of Results.

The People Dimension

Working with and through people is central to accomplishing results in an organization and consistently offers the greatest challenges to all levels of management as well as to individual contributors. People who work in organizations are constantly involved in the task of building and maintaining alliances, teams, and commitment with others. They are faced with problems of

---

4   Kaplan and Kaiser (2003)

encouraging cooperation, productive collaboration, and support for ideas, projects, and a wide variety of initiatives and activities. Successful influence depends upon an awareness of the needs of people and upon developing the skill to deal with a variety of individual personality styles.

People who focus primarily on this dimension are typically described as friendly, cooperative, supportive, people-oriented, etc. As with the Task Dimension, certain personality characteristics predispose people to behave in predictable ways in relation to other people over time.

Among the central skills associated with the People Dimension are:

- Supporting and encouraging
- Active listening
- Recognizing and rewarding the efforts of others
- Showing a genuine interest in others
- Building and maintaining trusting relationships
- Communicating and providing critique to help others see themselves clearly and to help them perform more effectively

As applied to the Cycle of Results, the People Dimension is also central to effective task accomplishment and is often referred to as the "soft skills."

Interaction Effects

Many variations of the grid diagram that follows have been used to illustrate the Task and People Dimensions as applied to organizational effectiveness. A person's position in the two-dimensional space defined by this template can be plotted according to his/her score (or position) along each of the axes. In reality, the distributions of attitudes and skills are generally continuous and follow the bell-shaped curve of the normal distribution, but it will simplify the discussion to think in terms of quadrants rather than continuous scores.

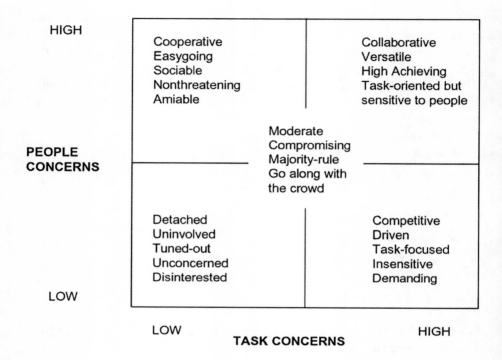

Low People/Low Task—Disengaged

The lower left quadrant of the template represents a tuned-out, uninvolved position that may be chronic in nature (people here may be low energy, depressed, chronically detached, etc.) or it may reflect situation-specific factors (disinterest in the present task, task not worth the effort, distracted by other things, etc.). People sometimes adopt this position as a survival technique in response to punitive or autocratic environments, as a result of outside problems, as a response to a stifling or boring environment, as a way to avoid making waves, etc. A person who consistently shows this style of behavior in an organization may come across as uncommunicative and cold or as docile and cooperative. The person may be highly security-motivated and consequently afraid to take a stand or may simply be unmotivated and trying to do just enough to get by. Whatever the reasons, this is an unproductive state. Little spark, creativity, or contribution can be expected from a person in this quadrant if the position is chronic. Obviously, a person operating with this attitude will have little influence or power outside of the narrow boundaries of that defined by the position.

A person may be forced into this corner of the template as a result of an autocratic (low people/high task) management style as well as by its opposite. The softer (high people/low task) style can stifle creativity and foster a bureaucratic culture that values the status quo and rewards good followers.

High People/Low Task Style—Overly Cooperative

The relationship-oriented person who values people is often easygoing, concerned with others and their feelings, and comfortable in a low-key, supportive, and nonthreatening environment. He tends to value relationships over the rigors and more-demanding behaviors associated with the push for task accomplishment. This is the high people/low task upper left quadrant of the template. People operating from this position are more likely to be concerned with the feelings of those around them and with their own acceptance by the team rather than with the requirements to get the job done. On the surface, this would seem to have great value in increasing their ability to influence and persuade others, but sometimes it has just the opposite effect. They usually aren't seen as strong players, especially in difficult times. This causes their credibility to suffer. Conflict is usually quite threatening to people with this orientation, and they will go out of their way to avoid it. This interferes with their ability to find productive resolutions to conflict-laden situations. As leaders, they are usually threat sensitive and often mistakenly assume that they can be "nice people" in all situations and that, as a result, others will like them. However, when taken to the extreme, leaders who focus too much of their time and effort in this direction will be seen as lacking in conviction and strength. People in this quadrant rarely take a stand on issues out of fear of hurting their relationships with others and/or threatening or alienating the boss (consequently damaging their social support systems).

Low People/High Task—Overly Competitive/Autocratic

The highly task-oriented manager who lacks a commitment to people and/or who doesn't feel that they need to be considered in the work setting may achieve impressive results over the short run. However, the factors that lead to her early gains are often the seeds of her ultimate failure. The dominance and power needs of results-oriented drivers often cause them to operate under a system of negative contingencies rather than from encouragement and positive reinforcement. The lower right quadrant of the template is often occupied by dominant, competitive Type A personalities. They are likely to be overly self-sufficient and to operate as closed systems as far as advice, counsel, or ideas from outside sources are concerned. Anxiety and insecurity sometimes cause their aggressive behavior.

However, another variation on this theme is the person who genuinely feels he is the best and the brightest. This leads to an egocentric attitude that others have little to offer because they're not as smart or effective. These people sometimes develop such a strong belief in their own superiority that they feel it is beneath them to waste time with the inferior ideas of others. Although such people may become adept at going through the motions of getting others to participate and even of caring for others, their underlying attitudes will ultimately show through and limit their overall effectiveness. Others often become quite creative in finding ways to passively resist and sabotage them over time.

People with the low people/high task style are often highly competitive and tend to see conflict as a win/lose situation. Their approach to influence is one of intimidation and sometimes of abuse of their position power. They rarely create an atmosphere that allows their subordinates to grow according to their potential. Some people who aren't internally confident have inordinate needs for control and tend to become anxious when they are not in control. In such cases, this internally insecure pattern can cause the person to behave in a dominant and aggressive manner when she senses a threat to her control. This tends to mask her feelings of inadequacy. Such people are likely to behave in a highly structure oriented, task focused, and people-insensitive manner.

Moderate People/Task—Quick to Compromise

The middle ranges of the template are where most of us reside most of the time. This moderate position is the most prevalent organizational style. It is characterized by compromise, going along with the crowd, being a good follower, and protecting the status quo. This is a democratic majority-rule position that would be preferred by a person with a strong need to be accepted yet with a strong enough sense of duty to recognize many of the task demands. This person will typically push enough to achieve results that are adequate and acceptable but not enough to stand out from the crowd. People in this part of the template don't want to be seen as rate-busters or to be out of step in any direction. They want to get along and meet all the demands of work and of people in an adequate, appropriate manner. They are survivors who are unlikely to assume high profiles. They typically seek compromise and workable solutions. They are conformists. Often, their influence with their peers comes from a perceived similarity. However, because they are not prone to take a stand or otherwise go out on a limb, their overall impact may be negligible over time. They strive to get along, not to rock the boat.

The middle-of-the-road management style is found in all organizations. It can be seen in great abundance in large, well-structured and predictable bureaucratic organizations. This style produces conventional, procedure-oriented companies that value compromise over innovation and predictability over spontaneity. Such organizations are not likely to be creative or stimulating places to work over time, especially for the more entrepreneurial and independent personalities. These settings will rarely encourage or tolerate the spark, conflict, and threat often surrounding and accompanying these types of people. Disruption is uncomfortable in the middle-of-the-road environment.

High People/High Task—Collaborative

A person operating in this quadrant does what is necessary to meet the demands of both the People and Task Dimensions. This high people/high task focus is necessary to achieve high-level results over time when dealing with serious and complex organizational problems, but it takes a great deal of time and energy. People in this quadrant don't see others in isolation from their responsibilities toward organizational purpose; neither do they neglect the needs of people while pushing for results. This quadrant represents the most difficult and demanding, yet most rewarding set of values, attitudes, and behaviors to maintain in an organization over time. People who stay focused on both dimensions often have great influence and impact. Think of Henry Fonda in *Twelve Angry Men* or Russell Crowe in *Master and Commander: The Far Side of the World*. Both of these movies show the ideal of this concept: a leader who never wavers from the demands of the task yet who meets those demands with compassion and understanding (although it may fall under the "tough love" category and seem harsh at the time). They demonstrate the ideal of the duality, and how tough it can be to maintain it.

Of course, no one can maintain this position all the time in all circumstances, and some situations don't call for this increased amount of energy and attention. However, those who make special efforts to remain committed to organizational goals through a focus on both dimensions have the greatest chances for sustained influence and successful impact. These people are most likely to develop their subordinates into effective team members and are most likely to remain open to the creative and innovative solutions that often come from unlikely sources. People focusing their energies in this part of the template are not necessarily charismatic or highly persuasive individuals, although the end result of their behavior will have a stimulating effect on those around them and will generate enthusiasm. They understand the differences between unhealthy, destructive conflict and the type of conflict that can be a positive force for creative problem-solving. They see conflict as a natural by-product of personal and organizational growth, and they can see the possibilities of new and better solutions from the productive resolution of healthy conflict.

They place a high value on people, but they aren't softhearted or fuzzy-thinking in their assessments, decisions, and actions. They are aware of individual differences, and they realize that a particular approach with one person will not necessarily be the most effective tack in a new situation or with another person. They are versatile and capable of modifying their behavior to meet the needs of their people while still maintaining their values and commitment to purpose. They protect both the People and the Task Dimensions while modifying their style and adapting to the new environment. They don't shy away from the tough and often unpleasant decisions that may be difficult today but are best for the person and for the organization over the long run. This requires that they develop and maintain a field of vision that is broad, deep, and distant. They find ways to attend to the demands of the People and Task Dimensions while moving toward personal and organizational goals.

One Best Way?

So, does this mean that there is really one best way to operate in an organization? Or does it depend on the situation? Should a person's style of behavior remain consistent, or is it possible to modify it based on the current circumstances? This is a long-running debate in leadership and organizational behavior literature.[5] There has been some recent theory and research[6] that describes the downsides of focusing too strongly on one or both dimensions. It appears that there may be some optimal level that is less than the maximum for each factor. However, this debate is likely to continue for quite some time.

Keep in mind the difference between behavior (which depends on personality, attitudes, skills, motivations, and the person's assessment of the situation) and the attitudes themselves (which depend on learning and values). There is indeed one best way in terms of the attitudes necessary for long-term success in an organization, but there are a wide range of appropriate behaviors a person can and should employ to handle situational contingencies. The person's insight and versatility determine the range of options she will have in any particular set of circumstances.

To maximize a person's influence and organizational impact, she must attend effectively to both dimensions. The highly production-centered, results-directed task master who places relatively little value on people may be able to come off as caring and empathetic for a while, but the veneer will eventually chip away, and she will ultimately be seen as manipulative, self-centered, and untrustworthy.

---

5   e.g., Blake and Mouton (1985) vs. Blanchard (1982)

6   Kaplan and Kaiser (2003)

Likewise, the person with a high concern for people and only minimal task concerns may be forced or frightened into an authoritarian display once in a while, but he usually won't be able to back up threats of greater discipline or to maintain this stance over time without considerable external pressure.

Early in a person's career, understanding the technical requirements of the task and focusing on individual production are important. In other words, he must be able to focus effectively on the Task Dimension. As a result of technical competence, he may be considered for managerial responsibility or for higher-impact technologist positions requiring greater interpersonal insight and skill. As he moves up, the People Dimension assumes greater importance. The highest-impact positions require that an individual demonstrate a high level of competence along both dimensions. The hard skills open the door and get you to a certain point of success. The soft skills allow you to consolidate your gains and open the door for continued and greater success.

Self-Management: The Integrating Dimension

The successful negotiation of the demands of the People and Task Dimensions is dependent on successful self-management. This starts with the "know thyself" adage. Not having self-insight is like trying to fly an airplane with no engine gauges to monitor its internal condition and no external sensors to report on its altitude or on the weather conditions.

But insight without appropriate action does nothing to help you achieve results. Some people are naturally more reflective and introspective than others, but all people can become more aware of the impact of their behavior on the organization. With the proper incentives, instruction, and effort, people can change their behavior in ways to help them achieve more positive outcomes. Understanding and managing our emotions is difficult for most of us, and people who are naturally more intense, anxious, or excessively driven often have more difficulties doing this. But it is still possible with the appropriate motivation, data, and coaching.

Although many systems of multi-rater feedback (often referred to as 360-degree ratings) eventually suffer from grade inflation (anything less than an "excellent" may harm a career) and from politics (e.g., "you scratch my back..." or "I know who you are..."), they can still be valuable sources of data about our behavior and its impact. Career developmental psychological assessment, competent professional coaching, and personality inventory data also can provide valuable information for insight and self-correction. In some lucky cases, a person may have a boss or colleague who is adept at pointing out the positive and potentially negative impact we have on those around us. The best insights are from multiple sources. Pay attention to recurring themes and implications, especially when you see them from a variety of directions. For instance, if you receive assessment results or personality inventory data that suggest that you are an agreeable, affable person, and if your 360 comes in with high marks on cooperation, and if your boss, friend, or coach suggests that others may take advantage of your good nature, then the chances are quite good that your personal fence rule (that is, what you should do when you're on the fence about whether to push ahead more aggressively or to hold back when facing any given situation) should be the former. You probably need to find effective ways to move your behavior on the Task Dimension a little farther to the right (while still keeping the good parts of your high People Dimension focus).

Summary

Work is accomplished according to a predictable sequence in organizations.

- The goal is of primary importance. To increase your level of influence, you need to show results. To achieve results, you always need to know your purpose—what you're trying to do. When trying to lead a group, the goal should be clear, stimulating/motivating, reachable, and time bound.

- The other steps in the Cycle of Results are:

  o Planning. After the goal has been established, we need to know how we're going to accomplish it.

  o Facilitating. This includes helping others to achieve results defined by the goal and plan. It is central to teamwork.

  o Monitoring. To ensure that the proper results are accomplished, one must be able to give and receive accurate feedback. There need to be effective lines of communication both ways.

  o Controlling. Depending on the feedback from the monitoring process, adjustments may be needed along the way. This is the essence of managing performance, and it is an active, not passive, approach.

  o Completing. There should be a process of closure that involves celebrating success and reinforcing good performance. There should also be an analysis of what went well and what should be improved upon next time.

The Foundations of Credibility.

- The Task Dimension is the continuing focus on the accomplishment of results. It is what keeps us aware of the goal.

- The People Dimension is equally as important. If we don't pay attention to relationships, we'll have little influence. This factor is what enables us to work together toward our common objective—the accomplishment of the goal.

- Self-Management completes the base that supports the goal. We are more successful when we understand ourselves, monitor our impact on those around us, and modify our behavior accordingly to increase our influence.

- The Task, People, and Self-Management Dimensions provide a stable support base for accomplishing our goals, both organizational and personal. They're like the three legs of a stool. If they're sound and sturdy, they carry the weight of the goal and focus the efforts to achieve it.

CHAPTER 2

A Widely Shared Obstacle

The Developmental Needs of Successful and High-Potential Leaders

Clients often ask us to review our assessments of their people to uncover recurring developmental themes so that the organization might realize the greatest return on their training and development efforts. The process of gathering such data involves not only a comparison of the average profiles of the personality inventory and cognitive test results of their people, but a content analysis of the developmental suggestions offered in the assessments. After analyzing several thousand assessments of successful senior executives and people in various fast-track leadership developmental programs, we clustered the most frequently mentioned suggestions for improvement into the dimensions listed in the Appendix. These include such factors as strategic thinking, organization, overconfidence, stress management, and general leadership. The two most frequently diagnosed developmental needs of high-potential and successful people fall clearly under the soft skills heading. These clusters share many similarities, but the first one reflects a tendency to hesitate and underreact while the second has more of an active, abrasive, overly reactive quality.

- **Influence and persuasion.** The recommendations under this category typically focus on poor communication skills; tendencies to undersell (or to sell ineffectively); general self-presentation; introversion or shyness; a lack of assertiveness; talking too much or too little; marginal boardroom presence; underdeveloped listening skills; not pushing for one's advantage when it would be appropriate to do so; tendencies to be too agreeable; etc.

- **Interpersonal insensitivity.** The developmental suggestions and observations here have to do with being too dominant, intense, or impatient; potential stubbornness; tendencies to push people too hard; being too competitive; lacking insight and political sensitivity; being overly wary, suspicious, serious, or critical; being insensitive or unsympathetic; ignoring interpersonal or emotional issues; being overly tough-minded, etc.

This pattern is typical of all groups we have studied. The two most frequently seen needs for development are the soft skills of persuasion/influence and interpersonal sensitivity. For instance, consider the following research findings.

- Among the top officers and executives of a Fortune 25 company, almost 70 percent were diagnosed as having deficits in interpersonal sensitivity, and over 60 percent were seen as lacking effective skills of influence/persuasion.

- An assessment of a fast-track executive development program in a similar company revealed that over 90 percent of these high-potential people had gaps in interpersonal sensitivity, and about 50 percent had deficiencies in their skills of influence.

- About 55 percent of the high-potential people selected for a fast-track program in another Fortune 100 organization were seen as having gaps in sensitivity, while almost 50 percent of them needed help in the influence skills.

- Among a group of hospital CEOs and executives, about 35 percent were diagnosed as deficient in sensitivity, and almost 45 percent were lacking in the skills of influence.

If this is true among exceptionally successful people and among those seen as having strong leadership potential, the situation is even more acute with people in the ranks, with technologists, and with people early in their career trajectories.

People achieve success early in their careers by developing one or a number of specialized task-accomplishment skills. These may be in finance, engineering, general business, software, or any other specialized area. These are the skills of the Task Dimension. Success in these areas then leads to other opportunities and to advancement into higher positions. However, with greater responsibility comes greater complexity and the need for additional skills. The soft skills of persuasion, influence, and interpersonal sensitivity assume greater importance as a person deals with the increasing complexities of management and leadership. Task skills enable a person to be successful early in a career and in a technically specialized career, but interpersonal skills allow him or her to be effective as he/she moves up and broadens into more generalized positions. To restate an observation from the last chapter, hard skills get you there but don't take you to your full potential. Soft skills enable you to get beyond the hard skills plateau.

Why Is This an Issue?

- Rule One of survival and success in organizations is this: Your job is to make your boss look good and to build trust and credibility in the organization. Assuming you have the appropriate hard skills and have been able to apply them effectively up to this point, the soft skills are the key to success in Rule One.

- To whatever extent you don't influence the process, someone else will, and that person may not have your best interests at heart. The skills of interpersonal sensitivity and persuasion give you greater power to shape your environment and get what you want from it.

- In spite of what many of us were taught, our work doesn't always speak for us. Some lucky and talented people may get discovered purely on the strength of their work, but that usually doesn't happen.

- It's hard to tell what people really contribute in an organizational structure. Large organizations tend to diffuse responsibilities and accountabilities. Soft skills help communicate a person's value and good works to others. But be careful not to oversell.

- Politics (the strategies people use in groups to get what they want) are a part of all organizations. It's a fact of life. Influence skills help you maintain a competitive advantage. The absolute truth is that all groups are competitive, and those who compete most successfully get more of the goodies.

- The person who is usually most important for your career development is not your boss…it's his or her boss. You need to make sure you have appropriate visibility so people can see and appreciate what you contribute.

- Unfortunately, the universe doesn't care about you or your success! Life in organizations isn't fair. We need to get over the notion that it is. One of the realities of life is that the organization (your boss) has power and is ultimately in control. To maximize your chance for happy outcomes, you need to have the ability to influence the process.

Why Are Influence Skills in Such Short Supply?

There are many forces that may interfere with our ability to persuade and influence others and to develop the necessary insights to help us reach our potential within our organizations. Among them are:

- Early socialization. We're taught not to blow our own horn: don't brag; let your work speak for you; it's impolite to tell people about your successes and talents; don't show off; etc.

- Lack of visibility. We think people pay more attention to us than they do in reality.[1] While this is good news for the majority of us who would rather have a root canal than speak in public, it also means that we think we communicate a lot better than we do in reality. People just have other things on their minds that keep them from hearing what we think are clear messages. We're not nearly as transparent to others as we believe.

- Values. Many people still have negative perceptions of salespeople and of "selling" in general. This is especially the case among technologists, who are often among those most in need of persuasive skills, but who don't value them. These negative perceptions color our attempts to persuade and influence others. Many, if not most, of us were taught that hard work is all that counts, and that we shouldn't have to sell ourselves. We want to believe that the facts will speak for themselves, and that our good works and extra efforts will speak for us. Then there are those of us who feel that once we've presented our ideas or solutions, others should be able to see their value; that our work is done, and that we shouldn't have to sell them. Some people do not have the ambition to scale the corporate heights. They choose to focus their energies elsewhere. They tend not to pay a great deal of attention to the development of influence skills. There are a variety of values and attitudes that keep us from maximizing our influence potential. In the case where values interfere, our strong suggestion is to change your mind-set. Realize that it's OK to sell yourself, your ideas, and your accomplishments. In fact it's necessary that you learn to do it effectively, because it will enable you to use your talents more effectively, maximize your performance, help the organization grow and prosper, and increase your chances of making a difference in general.

- Personality characteristics. One of the most basic human traits is that of extraversion/introversion. This concept will be described in greater detail shortly, but suffice it to say that extraverts typically find it more natural and normal to engage in the behaviors related to persuasion and influence than introverts do. However, on the other side of the scale, extraverts can overstep their boundaries and may not realize their negative impact on those around them.

---

1   Savitsky, Epley, and Gilovich (2001)

- Comfort level and self-confidence.

   o   This may be a fear of performing in front of groups. The fear of speaking in front of even small groups is very common, even among seasoned executives. However, it may also reflect a fear of failure and of being "found out." This can help fuel the effort and alertness needed to advance in a career, but it can also keep a person from approaching others with the confidence and self-assuredness to be persuasive and to reach out to others with solutions and ideas.

   o   On the other hand, an excess of confidence also can work against a person's long-term success if it leads to overcommitment. Over time, failure to perform as promised erodes a person's credibility.

   o   Many of us are just not that confident or comfortable trying to get others to do the things we want them to do. Whatever the causes, the idea of asking others to change their behavior, to do us a favor, to give us a raise, to give us a job, to choose our ideas, is truly uncomfortable.

   o   In those cases where a person is overly anxious or uncomfortable behaving in certain ways (e.g., trying to persuade others to do something or to accept certain points of view), there are techniques which can work quite well when administered by competent professionals. Therapeutic processes such as systematic desensitization and rational/cognitive therapy have been very effective in helping people overcome phobias and self-defeating attitudes. In the hands of a skilled coach or therapist, such techniques can be quite helpful to teach people to be more effective in their interactions with others and to present themselves and their ideas in such a way that they begin to have greater confidence and impact.

- Lack of insight or political savvy. Some people are just naturally politically naïve and flat-footed. They don't sense subtle political undercurrents that can give them clues as to the best timing and types of approaches to increase the likelihood of being able to persuade, convince, or influence others in their organization.

- Self-concept. Many of us have the sense that we're just not that persuasive. We see ourselves that way and consequently we don't make the effort to develop the skills and insights that would help us to have greater influence.

- Lack of awareness. It sometimes just doesn't occur to people that they need to think about these things, much less make the effort to develop these skills.

- Lack of practice, skill, or seasoning. This is especially true of people early in their career trajectories and of people who have come up primarily through a technical route. Presentation skills can be developed with training, effort, and coaching. Almost anyone can learn to make a more effective case to others. Many introverts have become very effective public speakers through effort, training, and practice. Younger people early in their careers typically haven't had a chance to develop these skills and are usually very good targets for training that includes video feedback and professional critique. However, influence goes beyond effective presentation skills. Coaching and feedback on the wider range of influence skills is often quite valuable early in a career, because people often haven't given this idea of influence much thought before that point. As with any skill, practice is important. However, practice doesn't make perfect. Only perfect practice makes perfect. That's why it's so important to focus on the right things and to have good sources of feedback for self-correction in developing any new skill.

Although there may be certain generic recommendations that can help anyone who wants to increase her level of influence in an organization, this is not a one-size-fits-all deal. Developmental plans will be different, depending on the unique mixture of skill gaps, personality attributes, and values and attitudes. People who enjoy interacting with others and who generally value the ability to persuade and influence others will benefit from programs tailored to help develop their insights about the most effective ways to present information and to make sure they are appropriately sensitive to their target audiences, not from programs that focus on changing their attitudes about "sales." And people who are overly anxious about presenting themselves and their ideas to others will benefit from help in becoming less sensitive to their fears and doubts rather than being taught the technical skills of group presentations.

Influence and Personality

Few of us are naturally gifted persuaders. We all have different combinations of needs, personality characteristics, abilities, skills, and values. One of the necessary first steps to develop or enhance a skill is to know where we're starting from and to understand why we're there. Self-insight is crucial for self-development. There may be many reasons why a person doesn't reach his potential for influence and persuasion and, depending on those reasons, the roadmaps to improvement may be quite different for different people. At the most basic level, we all need to answer these two questions:

- Why can't I influence people the way I want to?
- What can I do about it?

To help answer them, it will be useful to begin with self-insight. As a start, fill out the following brief questionnaire.

There aren't any right or wrong answers. Be objective—neither brutal nor overly rosy. It may also help to have a few people who know you, rate you. Check all those items that describe you. There are obviously some overlaps and redundancies here, but don't overanalyze. Go with your first response.

___I talk more than most people.

___People say I'm friendly.

___I enjoy social gatherings.

___I would rather work closely with others than work in relative isolation.

___I meet people easily.

___Others seem to warm up to me quickly.

___I will often take the initiative in a social situation.

___Some people may think I'm loud and uninhibited.

___I enjoy talking with all types of people.

___I'm more outgoing than most other people.

___I'm usually energetic and enthusiastic when I'm with others.

___I have little difficulty being with others.

___I enjoy small talk.

___If I'm frustrated, anxious, or in a bad mood, it helps to be with other people.

___When something good happens, I like to be with others to celebrate.

___**Total Score (number of check marks)**

1–3:	Strongly introverted
4–6:	Moderately introverted
7–9:	Mid-range
10–12:	Moderately extraverted
13–15:	Strongly extraverted

The Trait of Extraversion

If you're in the introverted direction, your fence rule (what you should do when you're on the fence, wondering if you should be more assertive or if you should back off) should be *act*. You'll usually be more effective by pushing rather than holding back. However, if you're extraverted, your fence rule should be to hold back and gather a little more data. Your risk is in acting too quickly, overstepping your boundaries, or saying too much.

This is obviously not an in-depth personality assessment, but the items above are the types included in most scales measuring one of the most fundamental personality characteristics—the trait of extraversion. It has been recognized throughout history. When you boil down any well-constructed personality inventory by a statistical technique called factor analysis, extraversion is the first global or higher-order factor that emerges. It is the first personality dimension in the Five Factor Theory (also known as the "Big 5"), a model of personality structure that is a well-researched and widely agreed-upon comprehensive description of the basics of personality.[2] It is also the first dimension in the Myers-Briggs Type Indicator,[3] probably the most widely used measure of personality for self-insight and team building, as well as many other well-researched and validated measures of personality used for selection and development.[4]

Extraverts are typically externally oriented, more prone to focus on people and on events outside themselves. They are inclined to be more outgoing, actively involved with people, assertive, and sociable. Introverts are more internally focused and likely to pay more attention to their own thoughts, ideas, feelings, and values. This is a trait, a long-term and enduring pattern of behavior that affects us consistently over time and in a wide range of circumstances. It is central to our personalities and to who we are as individuals. Extraverts typically find it naturally easier to do some of the things that help them to influence and persuade others than introverts do.

---

2   Barrick and Mount (1991)

3   Myers and McCauley (1985)

4   Haygood and Golson (2001)

Introverts can be quite persuasive, but they usually have to work harder at it, and they usually find ways to compensate for their natural tendency to be understated and somewhat socially low-key. Ironically, introverts sometimes do quite well in sales roles handling large, complex accounts where patience and a liking for complexity and analysis are rewarded. They tend not to fare as well in cold-calling environments that reward more of an outgoing, sociable, and assertive approach. Introverts tend to size up a situation quietly and offer solutions only after they've had time to think about the situation. Although they can often offer very good solutions, they tend to do it quietly and tend not to repeat themselves. Therefore, in a roomful of extraverts, where the chatter level is usually high, they can be overlooked relatively easily. Extraverts tend to offer their ideas and opinions freely and as a matter of course, while it sometimes takes encouragement to coax introverts into putting their ideas on the table in a manner that will get them noticed and considered.

However, being an extravert is no guarantee that a person will be persuasive. We've all known people who are outgoing, loud, and boisterous…and from whom we wouldn't buy toilet paper. Extraversion predisposes a person to interact with others, but it doesn't follow that those interactions will be successful. Some extraverts are insensitive and completely lacking in insight. As a rule, introverts listen better than extraverts (if for no other reason than they don't talk as much).

If you're naturally extraverted, you should monitor your impact on the group. Are you prone to overstep your boundaries, talk too much, act in an overly assertive manner, or otherwise impose yourself on others? If you're naturally introverted, you need to make sure you can wind yourself up to reach out to others when necessary. Remain aware of the positive aspects of this trait and how they can help you in your attempts to influence and persuade.[5] Are you too likely to sit back when you know you have something to offer, take a backseat to the more flashy but ill-informed players, or otherwise hesitate when you could have a greater impact on the thinking or direction of the group?

Emotional Intelligence

The concept of "EQ" (emotional quotient) as something vastly different from "IQ" (intelligence quotient) has gained popularity in recent years, possibly in part due to the realization that many competent people lack the skills of influence and persuasion. Some people have even claimed that it is a more powerful predictor of success than general intelligence. But the research suggests that this is not

---

5   Laney (2002)

the case.[6] The concept of social intelligence was formally presented almost one hundred years ago.[7] It has been described as a subset of general intelligence and also as a separate "intelligence" by various researchers, and some see emotional intelligence as a subset of this broader concept. More recently, Daniel Goleman[8] popularized the term, and this is now a field that is gaining greater attention from academic researchers. But EQ is still more of an intuitively appealing concept than a truly new factor in human abilities. The research results are not particularly clear or helpful at this time. Although there is some slight evidence that emotional intelligence differs from the abilities and dispositions that can be described by personality and general intelligence, the picture is muddy.[9] Several studies suggest that this factor can be explained by general intelligence, extraversion, openness to experience, agreeableness, emotional control, internal anxiety, and gender (with women scoring higher than men). This being the case, emotional intelligence may not be a useful framework for the development of influence skills, since personality and gender are not easily changed. That is, if there in fact really is such a thing as EQ, it may not be any more changeable than IQ.

Although there is no standard measure of emotional intelligence and no agreed-upon definition, most researchers suggest that it consists of at least three components: empathy (being able to perceive and appreciate emotions in others, being able to put oneself in the others' place); insight (being able to understand others' emotions and their likely origins, being able to connect the dots in the larger behavioral/organizational context); and being able to moderate or control one's own emotions. The first and third of these individual components may be trainable to some extent. The field of nonverbal communication is directly applicable here. Canadian sociologist Erving Goffman's 1959 classic *The Presentation of Self in Everyday Life* was the cornerstone work in this field.[10] Now, there are many references for reading emotions and nonverbal cues, from quick reads on poker "tells"[11] to academic cross-cultural studies of the universal emotional expressions.[12]

---

6   Van Rooy and Viswesvaran (2004)

7   Thorndike (1920)

8   Goldman (1995)

9   Schulte, Ree, and Carretta (2004)

10 Gofman (1959)

11 Caro (1994)

12 Ekman (2003)

Summary

- Soft skills (e.g., interpersonal sensitivity, influence/persuasion) are necessary for a person to build on the early successes gained from the effective application of hard skills (e.g., technical, task-oriented problem-solving).
- Psychological assessment is a unique and valid tool for pinpointing developmental needs of people.
- The most frequently observed developmental gaps in successful executives are related to interpersonal sensitivity and skills of influence.
- If this is a problem with people who have been identified as high potential and who are at or near the top, it's a greater obstacle for the rest of us.

Most of us need to further develop our skills of influence and persuasion because:

- Your work doesn't always speak for you.
- It's hard to tell what people contribute in an organization.
- Such skills will help you maintain an edge dealing with the politics that are a part of all organizations.
- If you don't influence the process, someone else will (and they probably won't be looking out for you).
- You need appropriate visibility to those who have power over your career.
- You are the one who cares most about your success (maybe the only one), and these skills help you compete more effectively.
- The reasons that people typically don't have as much influence and impact in organizations as they'd like to have are varied but can be categorized as follows:
  o Early experiences
  o Values (negative attitudes about "selling," people with little ambition to move up in the company don't pay attention to this issue, technical people often don't appreciate it, etc.)
  o Personality characteristics (e.g., extraversion is associated with higher persuasiveness)
  o Lack of confidence (e.g., people who are anxious or threatened by the chance of rejection are usually not as effective)
  o Lack of political sensitivity

o   Self-image of not being persuasive

o   Lack of awareness

o   Lack of experience, practice, or skill (e.g., younger people may not have had a chance to think about or develop their abilities to persuade and influence others)

- In addition to the assessment of the individual reasons for obstacles to persuasion, an assessment of organizational culture provides clues about the most effective influence strategies.

It is not necessary to be extraverted to develop strong skills of influence and persuasion. However, extraverts are more naturally inclined to interact with people, and this trait facilitates skill development in this area.

Although it is a popular and intuitively appealing term, emotional intelligence, or EQ, does not really seem to represent a newly discovered human aptitude. Many researchers conclude that EQ can be explained by a combination of well-known personality traits and general intelligence.

CHAPTER 3

The First Foundations: Characteristics of the Effective Persuader

A good way to begin to understand process of influence in an organization is to look at the nature of the persuader. This section presents some of the research and real world observations about the characteristics of effective persuaders. It covers the first two foundations of influence: credibility and liking.

Credibility

Psychologists have found that one of the most important factors in persuasive communication is high credibility.[1] The fundamentals to credibility are trust and expertise. This chapter can help you establish, maintain, and enhance your credibility.

The I-Competencies: Keys to Credibility

As noted in the brief description of these competencies in the introduction, peak performance in organizations depends on four foundation competencies—the I-competencies. The more capable a person is in all of these areas, the more likely it is that he/she will do good work, be perceived as credible, and consequently have greater influence and impact.

The Intellectual Competency

This is more than just how well a person can perform on a standardized test, although it does include the aptitudes that predict success in an academic environment. However, it also encompasses mental agility, quickness and creativity, depth of knowledge, and common sense. This factor is a combination of a person's unique mix of skills and abilities and how well she uses them. People who make

---

1   Zimbardo and Ebbesen (1970)

smart decisions and who use their talents effectively are more successful over time than those who make bad decisions and/or squander their intellectual resources. The data are quite clear and unambiguous. There are always exceptions to the rule (there are very bright people who never amount to anything, and there are people of very average intelligence who work hard and achieve at very high levels) but overall correlations between the components of this competency and performance over time are clear and consistent in a broad range of jobs and organizations. The more information, knowledge, and general ability to understand and solve complex problems a person possesses, the greater that person's credibility. If you can become a valuable resource for others, your sphere of influence will grow. This is central to establishing expertise, one of the two key cornerstones of building credibility.

The Interpersonal Competency

No matter how clever a person is and how elegant or elaborate his problem solutions, if he can't communicate them to others and convince others of their merits, it doesn't matter. People who have good social skills and who get along with other people are much more successful as a group than those who don't have as many talents in this area. They have greater influence in the group because others like them and feel good about them. The interpersonal competency is the key that unlocks the door of influence. It enables you to communicate the worth of your ideas. This competency includes general, social and persuasive skills, social insight and intuition, likability, and persuasiveness. These are the skills of the high end of the People Dimension described earlier. The intellectual competency enables a person to solve a problem. The interpersonal competency enables a person to convince other people that the solution is the right one. *As noted in the introduction, the influence subset of this competency is the primary focus of this book. Although a foundation competency, it is the most malleable and amenable to development through attention, effort, and coaching.*

The Integrity Competency

This is somewhat broader than the basic honesty-dishonesty dimension, although that is an important part of this competency. This is the cornerstone of building trust, the other of the two primary factors of credibility. This also includes general conscientiousness, discipline, and follow-through. The person with high integrity will meet his or her commitments in the time frames agreed upon and to the standards at or above those that are expected. If not, he or she will let everyone know in plenty of time so that they won't be surprised. Part of this competency includes the ability to focus and to use one's talents and aptitudes with appropriate discipline. This is the factor that holds things together and facilitates trust and consistency of performance. The greater the perceived integrity, the greater the trust, and therefore the greater the chances for being able to influence others.

The Intensity Competency

This includes energy, stamina, drive, and the person's ability to get fully engaged. People with high intensity are active, not passive. They are driven by a need to get things done and to see results. With the proper control and focus, people with high intensity will achieve at higher levels than those with only average levels of stamina and energy. This is the gasoline that drives the engine providing the fuel for achieving goals and for staying motivated in the face of obstacles. It is often manifested in an organization or team setting as general motivation. The more motivated you are, the more likely you are to achieve results, and consequently the greater your ability to influence others by virtue of your accomplishments and general credibility.

Other Considerations and Suggestions

Assuming one possesses the necessary competencies to maintain success and credibility, the following practical tips can enhance one's skills of influence and persuasion. These touch upon several of the other principles of influence that will be discussed in the next chapters.

The Law of Authority Is Essential to Establishing Credibility—It Is Closely Associated with Expertise

> **Factor A.**
>   0–3: Did you say something?
>   4–6: Eh…maybe…whatever.
>   7–9: Yes ma'am! (or sir).

People tend to see those in authority as having credibility. Although we may feel that this shouldn't be so, we have to deal with the world as we find it, not as we think it ought to be. We have very strong tendencies to comply with authority. Compliance with authority is often cited as one of the fundamental rules of influence and persuasion.

- The appropriate credentials help establish expertise. An MD with extensive experience in research and clinical practice is more credible than a CPA as a source of information about health care. This is a basic condition for influence—people need to know your credentials to judge whether or not your information is good. Your background and experience determine the credibility of your message. If you have credentials to verify that you know what you're talking about and if your audience doesn't know you, make sure they are aware of these credentials early in the process.

- If you don't have expert credentials, enlist the aid of those who do. If your audience learns that a leading scientist or management guru agrees with your premise, your credibility is increased. However, if you're personally acquainted with the expert, you need to make sure there's no appearance of collusion. People want their experts to be unbiased. If the expert has something to gain from the process, it will erode your credibility. You're more credible if a third party who doesn't have a dog in the fight plugs you or your message.

- Establishing yourself as a good source of information helps establish you as a subject matter expert and consequently helps build credibility. One of the best ways to do this is to develop good networks both inside the company and outside in the industry. It not only helps develop relationships, resources, and data that will help later on in your work inside the company, but it will also be of benefit if you find yourself on the job market later.

Image is important

- If you're not in a position of authority, you can do things to project an image to suggest that you are (or maybe that you should be) in such a role. One of the most practical and basic ways of doing this is to pay attention to your image. There is an entire industry based on image management. And don't forget the jokes (grounded in reality) that all you need to go anywhere in the organization is to look serious, walk fast, and carry a clipboard. Or that one's power is inversely proportional to the number of pencils in his shirt pocket. One's dress and demeanor are large parts of this equation. Don't underestimate the importance of image, but never forget that one has to eventually produce the substance to go along with that image.

- We're most easily influenced by people who project optimism, confidence, and a positive attitude. Pay attention to the way you come across. What are the nonverbal messages you communicate? Do people see you as upbeat and confident? Do they see you as tentative, hesitant, passive, negative, or overly low-key? Get feedback from objective outside sources.

- First impressions are important. You won't win the day by looking good, but you can lose it quickly with a poor self-presentation. Although people can recover from poor initial impressions providing they prove to be competent, it's much easier if you don't get off on the wrong foot. You just give yourself extra obstacles to overcome in doing so. Pay attention to the basics...eye contact, smiling, firm handshake, etc.

- Appearances are important in forming our perceptions of others. We like people who are attractive. Studies have consistently shown that people who are rated as more attractive by strangers are also given high marks on a broad range of perceived attributes.[2] Although few of us can look like Tom Selleck or Halle Berry, there are certain things we can do to look better to others. Dress is important in projecting an image of credibility and expertise. John Molloy, who wrote a seminal research-based book on the influence of dress on the perceptions of others jump-started the dress-for-success industry. Although last revised in 1988, his book still offers valuable insights into the manner in which people respond to others based on dress.[3]

- Dress up at least one organizational level. This helps you to communicate authority and presence. Although casual dress norms make this more difficult, it's still important to be perceived as similar to the people you're trying to influence.

- It's always better to be overdressed than underdressed, at least in business. You can always take the coat and tie off, but you can't put them on if you didn't wear them in the first place.

The Law of Trust

> **Factor T.**
> 0–3: You have a problem here.
> 4–6: Still needs attention.
> 7–9: Probably OK but stay watchful. This is crucial.

Expertise is one of the components of credibility. The other half of the credibility equation is trust. People need to know not only that you have the knowledge, expertise, or authority to provide good information, but they also need to know that you are trustworthy. This is absolutely crucial to being able to influence

---

2   Dion, Berscheid and Walster (1972)
3   Molloy (1988)

others. If you can't establish trust, or if you lose it, you'll never be seen as credible, and therefore never be able to increase your influence and impact.

The best way to establish trust is to make sure you're strong on the integrity competency. Unfortunately, there is a certain pull in some organizations for people to smile while outwardly agreeing but in reality having no intention of going along or following through on what they (seem to) agree with in meetings. Large, bureaucratic organizations characterized by turf sensitivity, silos, and rigid structures are particularly vulnerable to this phenomenon. And it's not limited to a passive resistance. It can also be seen with active attempts to do the other harm while putting on a happy face. "Grin-stabbing" is a more genteel way of describing this in a training vehicle than the usual corporate vernacular. But I'm sure you get the message.

Whether by grin-stabbing, failing to follow through, overpromising, or any number of other faux pas, once you lose trust it can never fully be regained. You may, with diligent effort, make up some lost ground, but you'll never reach that original baseline level of trust. Think of trust as a unique and peculiar asset in a bank. Every time you make a deposit to your trust asset base, it grows. But, once you make even a small withdrawal, the entire asset base is likely to be wiped out. The keys to making sure you establish and maintain trust are simple and obvious but too often overlooked.

Establishing and maintaining trust

- Always follow through. If you can't do what you commit to doing, let everyone know in advance. Never leave colleagues hanging. In short, do what you promise you'll do.

- Never betray a confidence, even if you feel no one will know. If you shoot your mouth off about the wrong things, word will get around.

- Never oversell or exaggerate.

- Never take credit for something someone else has done. It may offer a tempting short-term advantage, but once you establish a reputation of spotty trust, it will follow you to other positions. Your long-term credibility will be irretrievably damaged if you do things that cause others not to trust you. Never leave people in a position to be hurt by something you did or did not do.

- If you appear to be acting only in your own self-interest, you won't be able to gain the trust of others. This is why many successful salaried salespeople will find some subtle way to let the potential customer know early on that they're not on commission.

- Practice full disclosure. If there are flaws in your argument or other credible positions, acknowledge this before others have a chance to bring it up. It enhances your credibility and makes you seem reasonable, fair-minded, and trustworthy to point out some of the shortcomings or arguments against your product or position. Acknowledging on the front end that you understand counterarguments shows that you've done your homework and that you know the issues, but that you still believe you have the stronger position. Just be sure you have good data and analyses to show why your solution is still better.

- Communicate, communicate, communicate. Always keep people informed, especially if you have information that can have an impact on them.

- To build trust, you must trust. This means taking risks and being vulnerable to others. Obviously, if the other has proven untrustworthy, this is not a good strategy. However, in the absence of other data, assume innocence.

- You'll need to make the other person feel secure and feel that you have their interests at heart.

The Law of Liking

> **Factor L.**
>
> 0–3: Ever heard the term "brains-on-a-stick"?
> 4–6: OK, but there may still be some bedside manner issues.
> 7–9: You may have *too* many friends!

Think of the most credible and persuasive people you know. If you make a list of their traits and characteristics, not too far down the list will be something to the effect that they are likable. We are more easily influenced by people we like than by those we don't like. This means that you need to develop your social network within the context of your work environment. Socializing with people from work is important. By developing acquaintances and friendships at work, you increase the chances that people in your office will like you, and you keep yourself plugged into the grapevine for potentially valuable bits of information. People help those they like and avoid or actively hinder (or harm) those they don't. The more people like you, the better off you'll be in any situation. You don't have to be a screaming extravert nor do you have to spend all your time away from the office with co-workers. But when you have a chance to socialize with people from work, by all means take it.

How to increase the chances that others will like you

- We're more likely to listen to and believe people who we feel are similar to us. And we usually like them better than those we feel aren't as similar. We give them higher performance ratings.[4] We feel that those who have had similar experiences and who hold similar world views understand us. Opposites may attract (we find people who are different to be interesting), but we're more comfortable around people who are like us. This attraction is so basic that we're even more positively disposed to people who have names or initials that are similar to ours![5] Talk about your common interests and shared values when it is appropriate to do so. It will increase the chances that others will have positive opinions of you and will increase your level of influence with them. But be careful. This can appear mechanical or contrived if overdone.

- We like people who like us. As long as you really do like the other person, find appropriate ways to make that known. Sometimes the most effective way to do this in an organization is to mention to a third party how much you think of another person. In most offices, that word will get back to that person sooner or later, and it'll be more effective than if you were to approach that person head-on and declare yourself directly.

- We like people who make us feel good. Being cheerful, optimistic, and open with positive comments and feedback goes a long way in determining whether others like a person. Think about the people you want to be around. Do they criticize you? Do they constantly complain about others or about their bad luck? Are they cynical or otherwise negative? Or do they make you feel good about yourself, the company, the future, and life in general?

- We like people we spend time with. Familiarity usually does not breed contempt. Instead, it usually makes us like the person even more. Granted, this may not be the case if there was a major negative reaction to the person in the first place. However, most of us have had the experience of being initially negative or underwhelmed with a person only to find that with repeated exposure he grew on us and eventually ended up even more strongly on the positive side of the scale than if we'd liked him more in the first place. It's better to have the relationship grow gradually than to have someone like you, a great deal at first, setting up an only-way-to-go-is-down situation. If you want others to like you, make sure you hang out with them as much as appropriately possible.

---

4   Latham and Wexley (1982)

5   Jones (2004)

- We like people we associate with pleasant situations and tend not to like those we associate with negative situations. If you had a great time in high school or college, you probably still have friends from those periods with whom you stay in contact or at least think about favorably. However, if you didn't enjoy those years, you probably have little interest in keeping up with classmates. (Unless it's with a chosen few who shared your plight—misery doesn't love company; it loves miserable company. The "shared catastrophe" or "lifeboat phenomenon" tends to kick in with these situations.) All other things being equal, if you want others to like you, try to be around them when they're feeling good. If they associate you with positive things, they'll feel better about you.

- Although we like attractive people, we also like people who aren't perfect. (Think about Sandra Bullock in Miss Congeniality.) Showing others that you're aware of your own warts and blemishes makes them feel that you're more human. Self-deprecating humor is a powerful tool to make others feel good about you. You should take your work very seriously but don't take yourself that seriously. Be willing to laugh at your mistakes and clumsiness. We like those who show their humanity, not those who appear perfect or who try too hard to appear perfect. Feel free to make mistakes and to laugh at yourself. It'll make people like you and consequently increase your chances to influence them.

- Another variation on the similarity theme is that we like people who act the way we do. Literally, this means that if you mirror the behavior of the other person, they will tend to like you more. Experiments show that people who match the speech patterns and pace of others, and who show similar postures and gestures during conversation, are more well liked than those who don't reflect those behaviors.[6] This is part of the process of building rapport. The more closely you can match the tempo and expressional style of another person, the more likely she is to feel positive toward you.

- We like people we help and, somewhat disconcertingly, we tend to dislike those we have harmed. This is part of the phenomenon psychologists call cognitive dissonance.[7] We like to feel that we're consistent and rational. Therefore, we'll go to great lengths to fool ourselves into showing how our behavior and attitudes really are consistent. We need to reduce our dissonance if we hold two conflicting views of ourselves. For instance, if I do a good deed for a person, at some level in my subconscious, I'm telling myself, "That person must be good, or else I wouldn't have acted the way I did." And the

---

6   Dabbs (1969)

7   Festinger (1957)

reverse is true. If I wrong a person, even if I don't mean to, at some level I tell myself, "That person must not be so good, or I wouldn't have done that. I don't hurt good people." Our positive image of ourselves is one of consistency and rationality, and we'll distort our perceptions and explanations in many ways to preserve that image of consonance.

- In 1936, Dale Carnegie offered his observations and anecdotes about how to be successful in business and in life. *How to Win Friends and Influence People*[8] became a phenomenally successful classic and was a cornerstone for human relations training for years. Although revised since then, it still retains the feel of an earlier period when things may have seemed simpler. When people refer to "going to charm school" (sometimes with an underlying note of sarcasm), they're referring to the type of upbeat, positive approach advocated by Carnegie. However, while some may see his approach as a bit naïve, it has worked effectively for many people over many years, and most of his original observations have been validated by later controlled studies. And they're as pertinent today as they were then, maybe even more so. If you're serious about developing your skills of influence and persuasion, this should be high on your list of readings. Some of his basic principles for increasing the chances that others will like you, and consequently improving your chances to expand your sphere of influence, are presented below:

  o Don't be toxic—never criticize, condemn, or complain.

  o Show honest, sincere appreciation.

  o Find out what others want and help them get it.

  o Develop a genuine interest in people. We like people who like and are interested in us.

  o Smile. A smile communicates acceptance and liking. We like people who like us.

  o Remember and use the other person's name. But be careful. This can appear contrived if you are too obvious or mechanical with it.

  o Encourage people to talk about themselves and listen carefully when they do. Find out about the other person's interests and frame your conversation around them. Again, be careful not to make this contrived or mechanical.

  o Make others feel important. Minimize your own importance. Self-deprecation is endearing when not contrived.

---

8 Carnegie (1981)

o   The best thing to do about arguments is to avoid them. Even if you win, you lose.

o   Show respect for the other person's opinion and never say, "You're wrong."

o   When you're wrong, admit it quickly and emphatically.

o   Begin any potential confrontation or conflict in a friendly, approachable way. This disarms the antagonist and increases the chances that your ideas will be accepted.

o   Emphasize the points of agreement and similarity. Get the person to acknowledge agreement on even minor points.

o   Let the other do most of the talking.

o   Let him feel it was his idea.

o   Put yourself in the other's place. See things from her point of view.

o   Convey sympathy. Show the other that you don't blame him and would feel the same way if you were in his position.

o   Appeal to the other's nobler motives. In the absence of other information, assume innocence. Let the person know you think she is honest and will do the right thing.

o   Dramatize your ideas. Make them vivid and intense by involving emotion and presenting them with analogies the person understands.

o   Offer a challenge. Spark the natural competitiveness of people and channel it in ways to help your cause.

Summary

To be able to influence others, you must have credibility. Credibility is dependent on two primary factors: trust and expertise.

The I-Competencies are the keys to establishing and maintaining trust and expertise (credibility) over time.

- The Intellectual Competency allows us to develop the detailed knowledge and the problem-solving skills to develop expertise, one of the necessary factors in establishing credibility.

- The Interpersonal Competency enables us to function effectively on the People Dimension. The Intellectual Competency enables expertise while the Interpersonal Competency enables us to communicate that expertise in a way that will increase our level of influence.

- The Integrity Competency enables us to build trust. This allows us to meet our commitments, follow through, and work in a disciplined, conscientious manner.
- The Intensity Competency provides the drive, energy, and stamina necessary to achieve results and take care of the demands of the Task Dimension.

Establish yourself as a person of expertise.

- People in positions of authority are seen as more credible. If you're not in a position of legitimate hierarchical authority, you should at least project an authoritative image.
- Establish your credentials to emphasize your expertise or show that a respected and credentialed source agrees with your position. If you don't have credentials, find instances where those who do have them agree with your position.
- Establishing yourself as a good source of information helps build a reputation for expertise.
- Image is important.
- Dressing similarly to those in power increases the perception of a person's authority.
- We're strongly influenced by people who project optimism, confidence, and a positive attitude.
- First impressions count a great deal.

Establishing trust is directly related to integrity.

- Always follow through.
- Don't take credit where credit is not due.
- Never betray a confidence.
- Enhance your credibility and seem more reasonable and fair-minded by pointing out some of the shortcomings or arguments against your product or position.
- Never oversell or exaggerate. Once you lose trust it can never fully be regained.
- Communicate as fully as possible when you have information that will affect others.
- Take the first step by trusting that others will perform as expected unless you have disconfirming information.

We're influenced by people we like.

- It's important to socialize enough with co-workers to establish and maintain relationships.

- We usually like people who we feel are similar to us better than those we feel aren't as similar, and we're more likely to listen to and believe them.

- We like people who like us. Showing your positive regard for the other predisposes him or her to feel more positively toward you.

- We like people who make us feel good. Being cheerful, optimistic, and open with positive comments and feedback goes a long way in determining whether others like a person.

- Familiarity usually does not breed contempt. We like people we're around a lot.

- We like people we associate with pleasant situations and tend not to like those we associate with negative situations.

- Although we like attractive people, we also like people who aren't perfect.

- Another variation on the similarity theme is that we like people who act the way we do.

- We like people we help. Somewhat disconcertingly, we tend to dislike those we have harmed (even if we didn't feel that way before we harmed them and even if the harm was inadvertent). This is part of the phenomenon psychologists call cognitive dissonance.

- Dale Carnegie's original principles have generally been validated by later research and are for the most part as applicable now as they were eighty years ago.

CHAPTER 4

General Laws of Influence and Persuasion

Remember What Motivates People

The two principles of influence (credibility/authority and liking) discussed in the previous chapter are primarily focused on the characteristics of the persuader. This chapter is concerned with the basic goals that motivate people and the general laws of influence and persuasion that follow from them: authority, reciprocity, consistency, social comparison, and scarcity. To understand the best way to present an effective message, we need to keep in mind some of the basic goals that motivate people. We are all motivated to gain a sense of mastery and control over our environment. A useful organizing framework for understanding the keys to gaining that control is presented by Social Psychologists Robert Cialdini and Noah Goldstein,[1] which describes the following basic goals.

- We have strong motivations to perceive reality accurately so we can respond in our best interests. We need to stay alert and interpret things correctly so that we gain some advantage, or so that we don't lose something. This is the accuracy goal. It causes us to be alert to what others are thinking and doing and is an underlying mechanism for the influence of groups on individuals. We often look to others (authority figures or members of groups with which we identify) to figure out how they perceive and respond to things to get clues as to how we should behave.

- We are motivated to build and maintain meaningful social relationships. This affiliation goal is important even to strongly introverted people. Effective social networks are often literally the keys to survival. We tend to act in ways to gain the approval of others. This is a fundamental motivation. It explains why we ingratiate ourselves to others, and why we follow the norms of our reference groups. If we are accepted and liked, we have better chances for survival.

---

1   Cialdini and Goldstein (2004)

- We have a strong need to maintain a positive image of ourselves. This goal drives us to see ourselves as consistent. This goal of consistency explains why we will often go to great lengths to behave in ways we perceive as consistent. It also explains why we can be very clever at finding ways to fool ourselves and at rationalizing apparent inconsistencies to avoid the internal stress (cognitive dissonance) we would otherwise feel. Dissonance reduction is an important component in maintaining a positive image of consistency.

More Principles of Influence

There are two basic paths to influence.[2]

- The central (direct) route. This is where the person who is the target of the influence attempt actively analyzes the message and the evidence presented for it in a logical, rational manner.

- The peripheral (emotional, often beneath conscious awareness) path. Here, the target spends little or no time in rational thought before coming to a conclusion. Peripheral persuasion depends on our conditioning to respond to certain stimuli or triggers in an automatic way without taking the time to think and analyze. We're programmed to act, feel, or respond in predictable ways when encountering the laws of influence described in these two chapters.

The rest of this chapter presents the peripheral triggers that are so important to consider when crafting our messages and figuring out how we can make the most effective and persuasive presentations.

The Law of *Authority* (Again)

Although this rule was covered in the discussion of credibility in the previous chapter (where it was seen as being strongly related to the perception of expertise), it also belongs in the general principles. It is a fundamental and pervasive component of our motivational structures and a strong peripheral force in persuasion. Psychologist Stanley Milgram's experiments[3] provided frightening insights into the responses of normal people to authority. When people thought they were administering painful shocks to others and experienced severe anxiety as a result, they nevertheless kept increasing the (assumed) level of shock in response

---

2   Cacioppo, Petty, Koa and Rodriguez (1986)
3   Milgram (1974)

to badgering by the authority figures ostensibly in charge of the (bogus) research project. His research made it clear that people will go to great lengths to please and obey those in positions of authority. Therefore, if you want to increase your level of influence, you should do whatever you can to appear as if you are in a position of authority. Most people have a strong bias to comply when faced with authority. In Milgram's research, the authority figure was a "researcher" who wore a white lab coat and acted as if he were in complete control. Never underestimate the power of the uniform (or the dark pinstripe suit) and the trappings of position.

The Law of *Reciprocity*

Factor R.
> 0–3: And just what is it you seem to think you've done for me?
> 4–6: Maybe I do owe you something…can't remember though.
> 7–9: Oh you've done so much for me…*please* let me help!

One of Aesop's Fables is the tale of Androcles and the Lion. Androcles, an escaped slave, pulled a thorn from the paw of a lion. When he was recaptured and thrown into the coliseum to be eaten, his lion was the same one he'd helped in the forest. The lion, of course, purred and fawned on him and the emperor was so impressed that he released them both. This is the law of reciprocity at work. The lion was grateful to Androcles and reciprocated for the good deed.

People feel a compulsion to listen to those who have done something for them. This law of reciprocity is behind the strategy of sending out Christmas-themed return address stickers with charity solicitations at the end of the year. When a gift is included with a solicitation, it increases the odds that the target will comply. The examples of this law are everywhere. One often-cited example in the social psychology research and textbooks is that of the Hare Krishnas, a religious sect ubiquitous in the '70s and '80s. They could be found in all airports and at many public gatherings. A particularly effective technique they used to get people to listen to them (and then to donate to the cause) was to offer a flower to passers-by. They knew that people who receive a gift or favor, no matter how small, are more likely to listen to the request and to comply with it. This technique takes advantage of our strong need for maintaining a sense of balance and fairness. If another person does something for us, even something as seemingly silly and innocuous as offering a flower on a public street, we feel an obligation to do something nice in return. If you want to have greater influence with someone, do that person a favor.

This is the basis for our civilization, the idea of quid pro quo and fair markets. Social exchange is a general principle underlying much of human behavior: we expect something for giving something, and we are inclined to give something when we have received something. People have a strong need to keep the books balanced and are more likely to say yes to someone they feel they owe.

As one of the many possible practical applications of this rule to help you increase your own influence and impact, and with apologies to JFK, ask not what this person can do for *you*, ask what *you* can do for *this person!* Be the first to do a favor. This also applies in reverse. That is, people are typically eager to help others when approached in the right manner. It balances the books in their favor. But people respond better to requests for assistance than to demands that they do what you need them to do. "Can you help me solve this problem?" is far better than "I have a problem, and here's what I need from you."

This sense of wanting to keep things balanced also explains why negotiators come out of the gate with an extreme position. If you turn someone down on the first request, you're more likely to say yes to another one. This is the door-in-the-face technique (as opposed to the foot-in-the-door technique described shortly). For example, researchers[4] found that they were able to almost double the rate of compliance to a small request (complete a fifteen-minute survey) from people who had just declined a larger request (to participate in an hour-long marketing survey) as compared to those who received only the fifteen-minute request. If you've closed the door (rejected a request), you'll feel compelled to balance the books by complying with a smaller request, even though the smaller request may be far more than you normally would have granted.

The law of reciprocity helps us to achieve the primary goal of maintaining a positive image of ourselves and to maintain our social support network by keeping the norms of fairness and balance.

The Law of *Consistency*

Factor C.
0–3: All over the map.
4–6: Now they're starting to feel better.
7–9: All buttoned up. No loose ends here.

Alex Hawkins, a colorful NFL player in the 70s tells the story about coming home at dawn only to be stopped by his wife as he was trying to sneak in. "Where have you been?" she asked. "Well, I didn't want to wake you because I was late, so I

---

4   Mowen and Cialdini (1980)

slept in the hammock out in the yard all night." "Hmmmm...I took that hammock down six months ago. Can't you come up with something better than that?" she replied. His answer was "Nope. That's my story and I'm sticking to it!" He even wrote a book with that punch line as the title. This is pushing the boundaries of the law of consistency.

We have a strong need to see ourselves as logically consistent. We experience internal discomfort, or dissonance, if we perceive ourselves as inconsistent. The foot-in-the-door technique[5] (sort of the opposite of the door-in-the-face technique) is closely aligned with the reciprocity phenomenon but works because of the law of consistency. As the Hare Krishnas knew, if you get someone to agree to something, no matter how small, that increases the likelihood that she'll agree to a larger request in the future. We're likely to continue to agree to larger and larger requests if we've made smaller commitments in that direction. If you want to persuade someone to do something big, start with something small that's easy to do. Don't push for the close immediately. Rather, set the stage by gaining small commitments along the way. But the most effective commitments, those exerting the strongest pressure on the person to continue on their current course, are those stated in public. And, better yet, also in writing. Opinions that are stated in public are harder to change than private opinions. If you want to increase a person's commitment to any particular course of action, get him to talk about it in front of others. This is an effective technique used in weight-loss programs. When people commit to certain goals in front of others in the group, they're more likely to achieve them. It's also the basis for questionable car sales techniques. When the seller makes a low-ball offer, obtains a commitment, then gradually escalates the price with a variety of add-on and preparation charges, most people will continue to comply even though they may end up paying a great deal more. Although their gut may tell them they're being manipulated, they continue to play the role out to its conclusion to maintain their sense of consistency. Once you've made a (public) commitment, you'll continue to make larger commitments in the same direction.

We will go to great lengths to rationalize our actions and to see ourselves as consistent. This directly addresses our need to maintain a positive image of ourselves. The subconscious script going on in our heads is something like "I've agreed to these other things previously, so I must think this person and her ideas are good, since I'm a consistent person. Therefore, I should also agree to these other suggestions...otherwise I'll be inconsistent."

---

5   Freedman and Fraser (1966)

The Law of *Scarcity*

Factor S.
> 0–3: So what? It's everywhere.
> 4–6: Hmm…do you think it'll be available much longer?
> 7–9: Gotta get it quick…oh, my gosh, there's not going to be any left!!

We naturally value what is scarce, be it tangibles such as rare metals or abstracts such as secret information. This helps explain why we are more strongly motivated to avoid loss than to gain new assets. It is also the basis for the fear appeal. Our insecurities are powerful forces which drive our behavior. We fear being left behind, looking stupid, losing money, etc. And we want what we can't have. When we perceive something to be scarce, not easily obtainable or in danger of being lost, we value it more. Country and Western songs are known to hold more than a grain of truth about the human condition. Concerning the law of scarcity, look no further than Mickey Gilley's "Don't the Girls all get Prettier at Closing Time?"

Advertisers take advantage of this law by offering apparently lucrative deals, but for only a short time (This Sunday only! Only a few left!). Often it doesn't take advertising (remember Cabbage Patch Kids, Beanie Babies, and Tickle Me Elmo?). Unscrupulous salespeople have always taken advantage of this principle by creating false shortages in the mind of the prospect. For instance, when told that the particular car we like on the showroom floor has been sold, its value increases in our eyes. But, miraculously and by apparent heroic effort, the salesperson will somehow find one just like it for us *after* we've agreed to buy it if it's possible. In this instance, the seller takes advantage not only of the scarcity law but of the consistency law as well (we're more likely to follow through with commitments we've made in public). Ever been in an auction (or on eBay) and become caught up in the competitive bidding frenzy? The law of scarcity drives prices up, sometimes to incredible heights. This principle has been recently seen in the dot-com bubble, but it has a long and impressive (or frightening) pedigree.

The law of scarcity is what makes the snob appeal work. Not only will we try hard not to lose something of value, we'll pay more for things we think are exclusive. It is also the mechanism behind the success of certain counterintuitive moves by merchants. They sometimes find to their surprise that by raising prices, they sell more of the items in question. The implication with a raise in prices is that the item is becoming scarce and is in higher demand. Therefore, we feel compelled to get our share (or more) before the thing becomes unaffordable or is sold out.

The Law of *Social Comparison*

Factor SC.

0–3: Surely they don't care what other people think?

4–6: Uh…maybe we better see what the neighbors think.

7–9: The people we identify with help us to know how to feel and act.

Psychologist Leon Festinger, an early researcher in this field, first coined the term Social Comparison[6] in 1954. Others have used the term Social Proof. We look to people in our peer groups to help us interpret data. The *accuracy* motivation drives us to figure out what new information means so we may know how it can help or hurt us. People we trust and identify with (or people we want to be like) are a great resource to help us make sure we are perceiving and interpreting new data accurately. This is also the basis for delusional beliefs and behavior and for a mob mentality upon unfortunate occasions. There has been a great deal of research about the influence of groups on the individual, much of which was the result of questions about how seemingly normal people could have behaved so badly under the influence of the Nazis.

Our opinions are strongly influenced by those of the groups to which we belong or by those groups to which we'd *like* to belong. Notice how students dress like the others in their peer groups, from goth to preppie. On any campus, you can tell which groups students value by noticing their dress and mannerisms. And after a big win by the home team, it has been well documented that people wear more of the team colors the next few days. We have strong needs to identify with groups we find attractive and we tend to take on their ideas and behaviors without conscious effort or questioning. We tend to defer to authority without enough questioning in such circumstances, even with only a weak identification with the group. Milgram's experiments revealed that normal college students would administer what they perceived as painful, and even fatal, shocks to confederates in an effort to comply and please the person running the experiment.

Groups reward adherence to norms and punish deviation from the norms. People who identify with groups are more likely to tune out messages from people outside the groups and to listen more to people inside the group. The Jonestown and Heaven's Gate cult suicides are the extreme extrapolation of this phenomenon. As mentioned previously, we're more likely to be influenced by people we perceive as being similar to us than to those who are different. And people who are

---

6   Festinger (1954)

most attracted to or most involved with a group are least likely to be influenced by information that runs counter to the norms or standards of the group.

Participation (group discussion and decision making) helps to overcome resistance. This is a key concept in getting people to buy into a decision or program. If they have a sense of participation, and they feel they've been heard and their ideas have been considered, they'll be more likely to support the decision, even if it's not the one they would have initially wanted.

Advertisers tell us that this or that product is their largest and/or fastest selling. This taps into both the law of scarcity and the law of social comparison. If others are buying it, it must be good. And I better get mine before they're all gone (e.g., there's usually at least one toy or doll like the Cabbage Patch Kids that breaks out each Christmas season).

We can be persuaded not to trust our own eyes by peer pressure. Another classic piece of research conducted by psychologist and attitude change researcher Solomon Asch[7] showed that even when the differences in the lengths of several lines are obvious, the influence of others (in this case, colleauges of the psychologist) caused subjects to go against their own clear perceptions. We can even be persuaded that we don't feel as much pain as we should if others don't seem to feel it as intensely.[8]

When we see people looking up in the street, we usually stop to do the same.[9]

Ever wonder why there's so much money in a tip jar on the bar before happy hour? Salting the jar with dollar bills gives the message that other people are tipping a lot, and so should you.

In considering the influence of groups, it should be noted that a lack of support of even one other person can weaken the strong effect of majority opinion on other group members. Although this has been seen in research, it is graphically illustrated in the movie *Twelve Angry Men*, in which Henry Fonda gradually sways the other eleven people on a jury by presenting reasonable hypotheses and interpretations and steadfastly overcoming the objections and stubbornness of others during the course of the deliberations.

Summary

People are motivated to gain control and mastery over their environments. As a result, the following goals are important to us:

---

7   Asche (1951)

8   Craig, Best, and Ward (1975)

9   Milgram, Bickman, and Berkowitz (1969)

- The goal of accuracy drives us to make sense out of things, so we can anticipate whether they present threats or offer advantages.

- The goal of affiliation drives us to associate with people we find attractive and helpful. We seek their approval and acceptance.

- The goal of maintaining a positive self-image makes us strive for consistency. We will go to great lengths to appear consistent and to perceive ourselves as consistent.

The previous chapter outlined the characteristics of effective persuaders (credibility and liking) as the first two principles of influence. This chapter presents the other general foundations.

- The two routes to influence are the central (direct) path and the peripheral (unconscious or emotional) path.

- The law of authority is a powerful trigger. Milgram's classic experiments showed how normal people can be frighteningly easily manipulated into doing things they normally wouldn't imagine doing in the face of a strong authority figure.

- The law of reciprocity. We strive to keep things in balance. If someone does a favor, no matter how small, we feel obliged to that person and are more likely to help out in some way than if there were no obligation. This is a fundamental law that is at the core of our society. We operate by implicit rules of balance and fair play.

- The law of consistency. We are driven to maintain a positive image of ourselves. This is the basis for our need to appear consistent to ourselves. It is the basis for the foot-in-the-door technique and the reason salespeople try to get us to commit publicly that we'll buy a certain item "if they can only find one" before miraculously discovering just the model we thought was unavailable.

- The law of scarcity. We want that which is rare. Less is more. If we perceive something will not be available or it may be in limited supply, its value goes up for us. This is the basis for bidding frenzies at auctions, popular toy shortages at Christmas, speculative investment bubbles, snob appeal, and many other examples of seemingly strange human behavior. We are more strongly motivated to avoid losing something than we are by the chance to gain something.

- The law of social comparison. We're strongly influenced by the groups to which we belong and by those to which we'd like to belong. We look to others to figure out how we should interpret and respond to new or ambiguous information.

CHAPTER 5

Making Your Case

Presentation Skills

To be fully effective in getting your point of view across, you need to be able to articulate it in front of groups. This section offers practical advice to help you make your presentation most effectively, based on the general laws of influence covered in the last two chapters. However, if you have major problems, we suggest professional presentation skills training. Video feedback and professional critique are valuable tools for helping to develop effective presentation skills.[1] Although it's sometimes painful to see ourselves through these lenses, the facts are friendly. You can't improve until you know where you need to improve. Practice makes permanent. Only *perfect* practice makes perfect. This is as true in golf as it is in making presentations.

Do Your Homework

It's important to know as much about your audience as possible. An emotional appeal can be quite effective in some situations (e.g., when you're dealing with creative or emotionally intuitive groups like advertising firms) but can fall flat in other circumstances (e.g., dealing with an engineering firm where a rational presentation of facts and data is likely to be more effective).

- When the audience is friendly and receptive, when your opinion is the only one being presented, or when you want immediate change or action, present only one side of the argument. Don't waste time trying to look fair and balanced if you know they're on your side. If you present conflicting opinions to an audience that is already sold on your ideas, you risk confusing them and maybe even weakening their commitment. When you're preaching to the choir, reinforce them; don't open them up to consideration of alternative positions or ideas.

---

1   e.g., Linver (1994)

- However, if your target audience is likely to disagree, present both sides of the argument. This is also a necessary strategy when you know or suspect that others will present conflicting views or arguments. Show them you've already understood and considered the other viewpoints and that you've come to the reasoned conclusion that yours is the best. Of course you should have well-developed arguments backed up by data to bolster your position whenever possible.

- When you have a choice, go last if the opposing views are presented sequentially but with some intervening time period. This takes advantage of the recency effect—the last information we hear is likely to remain with us if the opposing argument was presented first, especially if there has been some elapsed time between presentations. However, go first if the opposing sides are presented in immediate sequence. This takes advantage of the primacy effect—the first information we hear assumes greater importance if all arguments are presented in rapid succession.

- Unless the target audience is exceptionally intelligent, don't expect them to connect the dots. More opinion change is likely if you explicitly state the conclusions for them. However, be careful when dealing with a very bright audience. In that situation, it's sometimes more effective to let them come to the conclusion on their own. Smart people want to feel that they've figured things out on their own and tend to resent anything they see as intellectually simpleminded or condescending.

- If your recommendations are clear and possible to implement within reason, the fear appeal usually increases your odds. However, if you don't have clear recommendations that can be readily implemented, a fear appeal can backfire. Again, people don't want to feel manipulated, and they like quick, direct solutions. If the audience perceives manipulative intent, there will be greater resistance.

- Whatever the advantages of your recommendations for the audience, your message will be more powerful if it is also accompanied by the knowledge of what they stand to lose if they don't listen to you.

- Your message will be most effective if you can show that they can get what you have to offer nowhere else. Exclusivity is a powerful motivator based on the law of scarcity and the fear of not having or losing something of value.

- People are more easily influenced when their self-esteem is low, and they tend to like others who show interest in them when their self-esteem is low. This partially explains the rebound effect whereby otherwise attractive and competent people quickly get into relationships with people (who would otherwise be seen as unworthy) shortly after the dissolution of a previous relationship. In the laboratory, people who have been made to temporarily doubt themselves find people who take an immediate interest in them to be more attractive than they normally would.[2] If you present your ideas to an audience that has been somehow shaken or made to doubt its ability, or to a person in a similar state of mind, your solutions are more likely to get a favorable hearing.

• Some people are easy to influence but can also be swayed the opposite direction with other messages. Don't congratulate yourself too quickly if the new boss thinks all your ideas are wonderful. Chances are he'll also be equally swayed by others who hold conflicting views. Such people will often change their minds and be overly influenced by the recency effect—the last person in his office will have the greatest clout.

• All other things being equal, the more extreme the commitment or behavior change you ask for, the more actual change you're likely to get (remember the door-in-the-face technique). The more outlandish the initial position, the more the other tends to reassess his own position, and the more likely he is to make a greater shift toward yours. And, if he has said no, he'll feel a need to balance the books by saying yes to something else. Here, you maximize your chances for a successful outcome by making your most expensive case first, then moving down the scale. If they accept your first position, so much the better. But it's important for people to have some room in which to operate, so always have a win/win fallback position (or two).

• Know about your audience's peer and reference groups. Our opinions are strongly affected by the groups to which we belong or to which we want to belong. The groups with which we identify exert a strong influence on our attitudes and behavior. People who identify strongly with a group are more likely to tune out messages that run counter to group norms or ideals. We look to others, especially those in our group(s), to help us interpret information accurately.

Making the Pitch—Practical Tips

These are some general and commonsense tips to make your presentation more effective. However, they're also fully grounded in the laws of influence.

• You need to believe what you say or your nonverbal (body) language won't match your words. Audiences can sense it when you're just going through the motions. If you don't feel strongly about your idea or position, it's probably

2   Walster (1965)

better to just keep your powder dry and save it until you have something you can really get enthusiastic about. Or, if you're naturally low-key, use the method actor's technique and get yourself artificially pumped before a presentation—e.g., run around the block (literally or metaphorically) to get the adrenaline going or think about something really exciting and positive right before going on stage.

- Your presentation to others should be assertive yet positive—you want to appear decisive but open and confident.

- Talk more about the ways your idea will benefit your audience than the technical details of how it will do so. More sales are won on an emotional pitch than in response to a solid data analysis, although this also depends in large measure on the audience. Emotional appeals are still important even to the driest of technical audiences. Have them think about what they stand to gain by going with your pitch and what they may lose by not doing so. Although it can be overdone and backfire with some audiences, the fear appeal can be powerful.

- Vary your cadence and pitch. And remember the power of the pause. We tend to want to fill the air with words. Tolerate silences. Give your message time to sink in. Let your audience have a little space to process these ideas.

- Smile and keep eye contact. This may be a cliché but in the midst of a presentation it's very hard to remember. If you're in front of a group, make it a point to look at individuals in the audience. Let your gaze linger long enough to make the person know you see her. Establish eye contact with everyone in the room if possible.

- Always know your goal—what you want from the meeting. This applies to a meeting with your colleague down the hall as well as to a formal presentation to the top officers of your company. Take a page out of the sales playbook—always have an objective and always find some way to move the process along in a positive direction. In a sales role, the ultimate objective is to get the order, but the most successful salespeople, especially those who handle complex large accounts, consider success a stepwise phenomenon. Anything you can do to gain a new commitment and to keep the process moving along is a positive outcome. But you won't have much of a chance for a positive outcome if you don't know what you're aiming for.

- Seek appropriate metaphors, analogies, and stories to personalize your message. Use clear and vivid examples to illustrate your position. People respond to stories. Do whatever you can to make your concepts tangible and to illustrate how the audience will benefit from accepting them.

- Keep the message clear and simple. Brevity wins. Get professional opinions on the use of graphics. PowerPoint presentations sometimes help, but they can also obscure the message. Stay away from what statistician and information design expert Edward Tufte[3] calls chart junk (anything that embellishes or decorates but doesn't clarify).

- Use humor but not the kind that pokes fun or appears hostile. And stay away from political humor. On average, you'll alienate half of your audience with anything blatantly or even subtly political. If you must make a political joke to illustrate a point (see above comments about metaphors and analogies), be sure it's nonpartisan. Use "politician" or "senator" rather than "liberal" or "conservative."

- Vivid, clear, and powerful examples are always more effective than statistical presentations. This is why politicians trot out individuals to illustrate their points and to personalize the argument (e.g., the family hurt by some governmental policy or commercial product, the war hero who supports this or that program).

- Consider what we know about primacy/recency effects:

  o   We remember points made at the beginning and end of the presentation and tend to forget what's in the middle so make it short.

  o   Make your point first if the audience needs time to think about things and last if they need to act or decide immediately.

- You will be seen as more credible if your target audience feels there is a common ground. A good way to help establish this feeling is to initially express some views that are also held by your audience. Again, we are usually more easily persuaded by people with whom we feel some similarity and shared values. People will evaluate you by what they think of your message and will turn off quickly if they know you're going to try to get them to accept a position with which they don't agree. In these cases, a stealth approach (establishing the rapport of common ground before presenting your message) can help. Of course, this can be seen as manipulative and is often overdone. Remember how you felt the last time you caught a salesperson desperately looking around the room to find something in common to talk about (a picture of your family, a sailboat, a golf course, etc.) to establish that there was an underlying commonality. Remember the first rule. A necessary condition for credibility is trust. And we don't trust people we think are trying to manipulate us.

---

3   Tufte (1983)

- Use the law of reciprocity. People will be more open to your message if you have done something for them, no matter how small.

- Use the foot-in-the-door technique. When people agree to something, no matter how small, they'll be more likely to agree to larger requests.

- Participation in group discussions helps overcome resistance.

- The support of even one other person weakens the strong effect of majority opinion, but opinions stated in public are harder to change than private sentiments.

Summary

Presentation skills are an important part of the influence arsenal. Training that makes use of video feedback and professional critique can help build these skills.

Do your homework—know your audience.

- When the audience is friendly and is likely to agree with you, present only your side of the argument. Don't risk confusing them or introducing conflicting data.

- When they're not likely to agree, present both sides of the argument. This makes you appear evenhanded and also confident that, although you appreciate the opposing view, your position is the stronger one.

- Go last if the opposing views are presented sequentially but with some intervening time period. However, go first if the opposing sides are presented in immediate sequence.

- Unless the target audience is exceptionally intelligent, connect the dots for them. If the audience is very bright, make your case but let them come to the conclusion on their own.

- The fear appeal works if your recommendations are clear and possible to implement within reason. However, if you don't have clear recommendations that can be readily implemented, the fear appeal can backfire.

- People are more motivated to avoid loss than to achieve gain.

- Exclusivity is a powerful motivator based on the law of scarcity and the fear of not having or losing something of value.

- People are more easily influenced when their self-esteem is low.

- The more extreme the commitment or behavior change you ask for, the more actual change you're likely to get.

Here are some practical tips for making the pitch:

- You need to believe what you say or your nonverbal (body) language won't match your words.

- Be assertive and positive—you want to appear decisive but open and confident.

- Talk more about the ways your idea will benefit your audience rather than the technical details of how it will do so. More sales are won on an emotional pitch than in response to a solid data analysis.

- Vary your cadence and pitch. And remember the power of the pause. Tolerate silences.

- Smile and keep eye contact.

- Always know your goal—what you want from the meeting.

- Use metaphors, analogies, and stories to personalize your message. Clear and vivid examples strengthen your message.

- Keep the message clear and simple.

- Use humor.

- Use clear and vivid examples to help make your points.

- Make your point first if they need time to think; last if you need an immediate decision.

- Establish a common ground with your audience.

CHAPTER 6

Sales School for Non-Sales Types:
You Need to Know What They Know!

Much of sales training traditionally has focused on territory management; planning a structured call; establishing rapport; showing the features, advantages, and benefits of your product; overcoming obstacles; and closing. Although a mechanical run-through of those behaviors can result in more sales with relatively unsophisticated products and buyers, it can make one seem shallow and manipulative when dealing with more complex situations and smarter decision-makers. When cold-calling, a consistently upbeat, cheerful, resilient, and optimistic approach is crucial to success. However, although these factors are clearly assets, it takes more than a pleasant and resilient personality and a set of sales techniques to consistently make an impact inside a large organization. When the message becomes more complex and when the audience is brighter and more sophisticated, the techniques that worked in the simpler environment can backfire.

When you have to work with people over time, some of the traditional sales tools will be ineffective or detrimental. If you're never going to see the person again and if your objective is to meet a high quota, you'll try most or all of the methods taught in early sales school to get the sale. It's a series of short-term battles and a sprint to the monthly quota finish line. However, if you use these techniques on co-workers, colleagues, or bosses, you'll look mechanical, shallow, and manipulative. Remember, trust is crucial for credibility (one of the absolute necessities to increasing influence), and people don't trust those they feel are trying to manipulate them.

So What Can We Learn from Sales Training?

Seek to understand. The concept of solutions selling, which emerged as businesses, technologies, and competition became more complex and demanding, has a great deal to offer. The first principle of this concept is that it is more important to understand than to persuade. In complex situations, an effective salesperson or

63

consultant needs to know her client's business, the systems supporting (or working against) it, the nature of his staff and colleagues, and the salesperson's own makeup to whatever extent is possible. The more you know about the business, pressures, technologies, problems, and desires of those around you, the more likely you will be able to help them. The more you help them, the more your ability to influence the process will grow. Therefore, you should first seek to understand. Data and facts are primary, crucial, and friendly. Many of the concepts used to gather information and to understand the client's world that are taught in solutions selling training courses are very helpful for further developing organizational persuasion power.

The obvious key to success here is listening. Without seeming contrived, you need to pay attention to the stuff taught in active listening training. This includes asking questions, restating the other person's point in such a way that you understand it and demonstrate that you get it, keeping your mouth shut until you're really sure you hear the other person, and not trying to push for closure too quickly. It's a cliché but very true: you won't understand the other person by talking. And you very much need to understand the other person to establish yourself as a credible source of help, advice, and counsel. Trusted advisers do a great deal more listening than presenting their point of view. Yes, there is a time to discuss your opinions, services, or solutions, but that time is usually later than you think, especially if you're an impatient extravert.

Know your goals. As stated in earlier chapters, you should always know what success looks like and have a goal in mind that moves you toward that success. Just as in complex sales, the immediate goal is rarely to "get the order" although that's obviously the ultimate target. Your primary goal is to get whatever it is you want from your own organizational context, but there will be many other sub-goals along that path. In the sale, the most successful people are able to move the process along in some way with each contact. Outcomes such as setting up a meeting with other people in the target organization to learn more about their needs, or getting a commitment from your prospect to visit another client to see how your system works, are clearly seen as wins. And anything that moves your cause along should also be seen as a positive outcome. But you need to know what your ultimate success looks like, or you won't know whether you're moving forward or treading water. As in so many areas of life, clear goals are important. You have to know where you're going before you chart a course for getting there. Any sales training course should have a clear emphasis on goal-setting.

Visualize success. Many training programs make use of visualization (another term for imagination) to increase the chances for success. This technique is used with great success in coaching athletes to help them improve and to help them achieve higher levels of confidence, skill, and performance. Simply put, it's the process of seeing yourself at your best. If you visualize a successful golf shot, taking the time to make it as vivid, realistic, and intense as possible while including all the good feelings that go along with success, you'll hit the ball better. And this applies to other areas of life. The use of mental imagery in coaching has a long and successful history, and it also works in business. If a person imagines a successful sale in great detail, the mind interprets it as the real thing. Therefore, without having done anything physical, the person's confidence is increased, because the mind has been tricked into thinking that the person has been successful. If you want to be persuasive, picture yourself at your best. Remember the times when you've been successful persuading others and relive those times as clearly, vividly, and intensely as possible. Also, visualize yourself being successful in other instances where you're trying to influence others. Although this is often best accomplished with a skilled coach, you can make progress here on your own. Remember the adage that whether you think you'll be successful or whether you think you'll be unsuccessful, you're probably right.

Practical tips: Here are a few more suggestions based on the things effective persuaders actually do to be successful.

- Know what you want to happen. Know what success looks like.

- Stay organized and make yourself keep things moving along toward your goal.

- Follow through and meet your commitments.

- Build and maintain good relationships.

- Keep others informed.

- Help people so they see you as a resource.

- Don't always try to push for the close.

- But do *ask for the order* when it is appropriate to do so. You need to let people know what you want them to do. After you're sure you fully understand the situation, and that you in fact have a solution, product, or service that will make the other person's life easier, let him or her know. But do so within the context of the laws of influence.

- If you continue to encounter resistance or obstacles after applying all of the appropriate principles, try asking the person, "What will make this better? What do you need for me to do?" And also realize that sometimes you just won't get the sale no matter what you do. But I promise, if you apply these principles consistently, you'll dramatically increase your hit rate—not only in sales but in other functional areas.

Other Applications of Sales Training Concepts: Focus on the Positive

Another concept closely related to that of positive imagery and visualization of success comes from the research on optimism. It provides insights into why some salespeople are consistently more successful than others; why athletes and teams of similar ability often perform very differently; why some organizations consistently outperform their competitors; and why some people stay healthier than others.

The emerging field of positive psychology got an initial push from this research. Until recently, psychologists have mostly studied pathology. However, a few years ago Psychologist and former president of the American Psychological Association Martin Seligman published *Learned Optimism*[1] which was one of the early works in this new field. He had studied how learned attitudes (helplessness on the negative side and optimism on the positive) affect our accomplishments and our views of ourselves. As the focus began to shift more to the study of positive processes and success rather than on pathology, researchers found that optimism predicted success in a wide range of situations, from sales to athletic contests to political elections. This reinforced earlier observations from psychologist and founder of the therapeutic school of Rational Emotive Behavior Therapy Albert Ellis[2] and others that the way we think about problems affects our emotions, and we can alleviate or aggravate negative feelings by changing the way we think.

In the realm of politics, Seligman and his colleagues were able to predict the outcomes of national elections with uncanny accuracy through careful analysis of nomination acceptance speeches. There was a clear pattern that the person with the most optimistic speech (and, therefore in most cases, the most optimistic and positive message) won the election. The results were unequivocal—people want to see a positive vision for the future, especially in tough times and negative circumstances. The people who were elected were the ones most able to communicate a positive, upbeat, and optimistic message.

Animal studies and research on people show that, when we perceive no control or hope, we become pessimistic. And that pessimism leads to depression. In short, we learn to be helpless. The first classic study of this phenomenon showed that animals in a cage that have become used to electric shocks fail to move to another part of the cage to avoid the shock when given the opportunity to do so. Once they learned that there was (at that time) no escape, they later shut down and failed to explore their environment when it changed and offered opportunities to escape. This set of experiments led to questions about how to unlearn counterproductive attitudes and behavior. If pessimism is a learned response, what about

---

1   Seligman (1998)
2   Ellis (1998)

optimism? Can it be learned? This research led to the finding that our attitudes about ourselves could be understood by the way we explain events to ourselves. There are two explanatory styles as described below:

The Negative (Pessimistic) Explanatory Style

Assumes that *bad events*:

- Will go on indefinitely (they're seen to be permanent)
- Affect everything (they're pervasive)
- Are my fault (they're due to me personally)

However, when *good things* happen, this style assumes:

- They won't last (time limited—impermanent)
- They don't spill over or affect anything else (specific—not pervasive)
- They aren't due to anything I did (impersonal)

The Positive (Optimistic) Explanatory Style

Assumes that *bad events*:

- Won't last forever (not permanent)
- Don't affect everything (not pervasive)
- Aren't my fault (impersonal)

And that *good things*:

- Will continue (permanent)
- Affect other things (pervasive)
- Are because of me (personal)

The ABC Model—Changing the Way You Think Changes the Way You Feel

To learn to be more optimistic, we apply the ABC (Adversity—Belief—Consequences) principles of rational/cognitive therapy.[3] This is a method for analyzing our beliefs about events and then changing these beliefs based on objective data. As the Greek philosopher Aristotle originally observed, and as modern-day research has verified, our thoughts and beliefs influence our emotions and vice versa. Systematically analyzing our thoughts and explanations and consciously

---

3   Ibid

challenging those that are irrational are key to changing our emotions. The process of the ABC analysis is outlined below:

- **Adversity**—The activating event: something bad or threatening happens. (For example, the boss chooses a colleague's proposal for a new project over our own.)

- **Belief**—What you think about the adversity; your explanatory style. (For example, "Well, that's to be expected…I'm not very persuasive…and besides, my idea probably wasn't that good anyway.")

- **Consequences**—The end result, not of the adversity, but of your beliefs about it. (For example, "I guess this means that the boss thinks I'm incompetent. My job may be in jeopardy now. I should never step out and give my opinion.") If it's a negative explanatory style like this example, the consequences are even greater pessimism and a further erosion of confidence.

However, to change the negative consequences that arise from faulty beliefs, we add the D&E components:

- Disputing—Challenging your irrational beliefs about the event and its causes. This involves an active process to separate the rational from the irrational. It often takes the form of finding examples to the contrary. If you can remember times when your ideas were accepted, you've disputed the belief that you're "just not persuasive." If you think about times when you have been able to influence the boss, you've challenged the belief that this outcome is to be expected. If you teach yourself to see that some of your negative beliefs have no basis in fact and actively seek alternative explanations and contradictory examples, you then begin the process of what psychologists call "cognitive restructuring," or changing the way you think about things. The active disputing of irrational beliefs is the key to changing your negative emotions and reactions to certain events. By changing our interpretations of the event, we begin to change our feelings about it.

- Effects—The new consequences resulting from a rational interpretation of the event. For example, a new consequence of actively challenging and disputing your irrational beliefs that you always fail and will continue to do so in your efforts to influence others is to accept the fact that although you'll lose sometimes, that doesn't necessarily make others think less of you, your job is not really at risk, and there are clearly times when you are successful.

Summary

There are many things taught in sales training that can help non-salespeople increase their powers of influence and persuasion.

- Some traditional sales techniques work only with unsophisticated audiences.
- When the audience is brighter and more sophisticated, it is important to understand as much as you can about the situation. Gathering information through the application of careful and focused questions is a key to success.
- Always know your ultimate goal and have targets that move you in that direction.
- Visualize success. The use of mental imagery is not only effective in increasing athletic performance but also in helping people build their confidence and abilities to be more successful in business, to include further developing their ability to influence the process.

The research on optimism shows that animals and people learn to be helpless (or to act as if they were helpless). Therefore they can also learn that their actions make a difference. This applies to our efforts to be more effective persuaders.

- A pessimistic explanatory style (how we interpret bad and good things that happen) is associated with depression and low performance in a wide range of circumstances.
- An optimistic explanatory style leads to happier outcomes.
- We can change the way we think about things by using the ABC Model:
  o There is an Activating event, some sort of adversity.
  o We have certain Beliefs about that event that cause our reaction. (The belief or the way we explain it to ourselves is what causes the reaction, not the event itself.)
  o There is a Consequence from our belief, often fear, anxiety, or pessimism, which can lead to longer-term negative situations.
- To change those negative consequences, we actively Dispute the irrational beliefs we have about the activating event.
- New Effects are a result of changing the way we explain things to ourselves, of changing our irrational beliefs through active, conscious challenging and disputing.

CHAPTER 7

Organizational Survival Skills and Practical Advice

Chapter 1 presented an overview of how work gets accomplished in organizations. Although that information helps to put things into a useful framework, it doesn't take into account the political nature of life in organizations. The theories and observations about work in organizations tend not to emphasize that most decisions are emotional, not rational, and that politics underlie much of what goes on. Politics are a fact of organizational life, and all organizations are competitive. The person who can influence others has more power and is more likely to be able to get her needs met than the person who does not, cannot, or will not exert influence. What follows is by no means a comprehensive roadmap for how to survive and thrive in an organization, but it can certainly help.

Your Organizational Culture

Organizations tend to develop distinct cultures that often determine the most effective ways to influence others within that culture. The culture of an organization is a powerful influence on people's ideas, emotions, and behavior.[1] As mentioned earlier, an emotional appeal may be wasted on a stereotypical engineering organization, which is inherently data oriented and likely to value reasoned analysis. And a numbers-heavy deck with complex charts and many statistics will usually fall flat when presented to creative teams such as are often found in advertising and public relations firms. Is your group inherently data oriented? Or is it more intuitive? More formal? Informal? Understanding the implications of your cultural context can help you make more effective presentations and can increase your chances for exerting greater influence within the organization.

Another aspect of corporate culture is that it tends to be underestimated as a deep and long-term determinant of satisfaction. If you're in a culture that is inherently uncomfortable for you, it won't be a good fit over time. Such a mismatch will eventually take its toll. Therefore, it's a good idea to periodically assess the fit

---

1   Pizer and Hartel (2005)

between your personality and your evolving needs and values and the organizational culture. And it's a very good idea to get some data about the culture of any organization you're considering joining before you make the final decision.

There are relatively formalized methods of assessing corporate culture through statistical surveys and similar metrics, but it can also be done quite well from keen and objective observation. To bring the picture of your own organization's culture more sharply into focus, look at who the stars and goats are. Who gets rewarded? Why? Who doesn't get recognition? Why? Do the leaders seem warm and approachable or cool and distant? What are the success stories people use when they recount the history of the company? What do you think of the people you work with? What are the social expectations? Do co-workers play and socialize together? What do these observations tell you about your company's values and culture? More importantly, what do they tell you about your fit within this context? Assuming that your fit with the culture is not a major issue (if it is, you need to explore this issue more deeply), what are the implications for influence strategies inside the company? Understanding your corporate culture helps you package your ideas in a way that will increase their chance for acceptance. This does not mean that you're sacrificing your integrity; it means you're increasing your chances for success.

Starting Off on the Right Foot

Think about the last time you made a transition into a new company or a new job. It's an uncomfortable time for most people. What did you do? What would you have done differently? Here's a list of things to do *next* time.

- Make sure you know what you're supposed to do and when you're supposed to do it. Remember Rule One: *your job is to make your boss look good and to build trust and credibility.* Don't rely on job descriptions and don't assume you know what the boss wants. Ask! It's eye-opening and sometimes frightening to see how much of a disconnect often exists between the way a boss and subordinate view the nature of the subordinate's duties. Most executives don't lay out explicit expectations, so this is your responsibility.

- Make it a point to introduce yourself to everyone; work on developing a social network right from the start. Take the initiative. Go to lunch with others, have coffee, chat, etc. Act like you're eager to get to know everyone. Even if this is uncomfortable and even if you're an extreme introvert, you can still behave as if you were more outgoing. It's a behavior, a learned skill. Not a personality transplant. Make yourself put on a happy face. Take this initiative, and it will go a long way toward establishing you as an interested and engaged new team member.

- Keep your opinions to yourself until you've had a chance to get the lay of the land. Gather information. Listen. Don't tell or sell.

- Never, ever trash your old company, colleagues, or bosses. If you are doing it now, people will assume you'll do it again.

- Be the first to speak. Say hi. Fence rule: "Should I say hello or not?" Say it!

- Play nice. Don't get pulled into gossip or backstabbing. You won't be able to build trust by getting dragged into cynicism or faultfinding. Cynicism is the refuge of the powerless. Stay positive.

- Be open and accessible but don't commit to one group or another until you know the lay of the land. Sometimes the most friendly people have their own agendas (they may be malcontents or slackers and see you as a possible ally). Stay neutral until you really know what's going on. Don't get locked into one group too quickly. This is a balancing act until you become more familiar with your new surroundings.

- Role models and mentors can be very helpful, but you need to find the right ones. They can offer valuable feedback and insights, but you must be able to stand on your own and to appear that way as well. As you progress and adjust to the organization, don't be overly dependent on a mentor.

- Look at who's successful in the company. How do they look, dress, and act? If what you see appeals to you, model the appropriate behaviors. Take a page from their book. Find out quickly who has the power in your organization. Not only who has position power (power conferred by organizational hierarchy) but personal influence power. Stay alert and aware. Where are the nodes of information and influence that can help you get your needs met? Think about how you can use these to your advantage.

- Try to find an early success. If you can identify a problem that needs fixing and do so in a short time, it will help jump-start your reputation and increase your credibility.

If you're going into a leadership role, pay attention to all of the above points but also consider the following suggestions about how to avoid some of the common mistakes.[2]

- Set realistic expectations. Never assume that your initial take on the situation, or the initial mandate and charter, is set in stone. Adjusting to a new political

---

2   from Ciampa and Watkins (1999)

context, new culture, and new set of mandates is a delicate dance, and things are rarely as they appear on the surface. Always make sure you know what success looks like in your new boss's eyes and be able to adjust and negotiate when you see that expectations are not in line with the reality of the situation. And don't commit to anything you can't deliver.

- Spend more time talking to others than reading reports. Don't isolate yourself. New leaders sometimes rely too much on financial analyses and operating metrics to learn their new organizations.

- Quick fixes backfire. Don't feel like you have to come up with the one right answer to fix everything right off the bat. It takes tincture of time and a willingness to live with complexity and ambiguity before you will really understand what's going on and before you see the proper ways to begin to address the real problems.

- Focus on clear, manageable targets in the early days and get a few wins under your belt. Don't try to do too much at once. You will overstretch yourself and your people, and you'll end up with marginal results because of too many goals and diffused priorities.

- Get a quick and accurate assessment of your new team. This is where psychological assessment can be of great benefit to a new leader. Don't stay too long with team members who aren't really on the team. Many times, leaders who tend to stay too much in the High People/Low Task quadrant give others the benefit of the doubt longer than necessary and tend to let others take advantage of their good nature. It's a mistake to shoot everyone and bring in a whole new team before assessing your inheritance, but it's an equally damaging mistake to live too long with marginal performers.

- As mentioned in the general points above, don't get captured by the wrong people. Everybody will have his or her own compelling story and will be jockeying for position. Don't take everything you hear as gospel. Get information from as broad an array of sources as possible.

After the Transition

- Know what you want. Too many times, we don't define our goals and consequently don't get the most out of our efforts or, worse, let those who don't have our interests at heart define the situation. Think about the outcome you need and stay aware of opportunities to move your own interests forward (but with the usual caveats about not hurting others and not appearing to be self-serving while doing so).

- Assume innocence. If we attribute bad motives to others, that can start a downward spiral. Assume everyone's trying to do his or her best with the tools and information at hand. If you assume that the mistakes are honest and not directed at you personally, your reaction to the person will be much different than it would be if you knew that person meant to do you harm. But don't be naïve. Always watch what others do and watch their nonverbal cues.

- Office gossip can be both valuable and dangerous.

- The grapevine is a necessary source of potentially valuable information. Pay attention to it but never forget that it's often inaccurate, sometimes incredibly so. Keep your eyes and ears open.

- Never, ever betray a confidence. Don't reveal confidential information, whether personal or about the organization. Along with satisfying your boss, your job is to build trust. You won't do that by having loose lips.

- Stay away from personal gossip; focus on business gossip. Personal gossip hurts people and damages reputations. It is too often planted and manufactured for political reasons. Avoid it. However, gossip about the business and industry are potentially valuable resources. You need as much data as possible, and this includes informed guesses about directions and trends that may have an impact on you.

- Assume anything you say will get around the organization.

- Be generous with your expressions of appreciation. Most of us don't take advantage of opportunities to influence the behavior of others by applying the commonsense and research-based principles of reinforcement.

- Even if the other person is seemingly incompetent, you can always find something he does well, or that you appreciate. Never pass up a chance to give someone positive reinforcement by expressing your sincere appreciation. Always acknowledge good work and success but don't praise constantly or it loses its effect. And don't praise work that is not good. That will make you come off as insincere.

- Although you can lose points by appearing insincere, and although you should avoid flattery, controlled studies have shown that, even when the targets know the other is trying to flatter, they still feel more positively toward him than would normally have been the case.

- But be careful not to make it personal (appearance, etc.). This can lead into dangerous territory, such as harassment complaints.

- Compliments and encouragement should be directed upwardly, laterally, and downwardly in the organization. If it's always upward, you quickly get the reputation of being a brownnoser. Pay particular attention to positive reinforcement and shows of appreciation downwardly. It helps you build a base of support and allies.

Working on Teams

Sooner or later, we all have to work with others in some sort of a teamwork environment. Therefore, it will be to your benefit to review some of the things we know about effective teams and some of the skills of good team members and team leaders.

The Characteristics of Effective Teams

Although there are many types of teams, the successful ones share certain characteristics. In one real-world research project that included several high-profile business, military, sports, and medical teams, teamwork researchers Carl Larson and Frank LaFasto[3] identified three basic types of teams:

- **Problem Resolution Teams** (e.g., executive teams) that depend on trust and have a focus on solving a variety of strategic and tactical problems.

- **Creative Teams** (e.g., new product development teams) that focus on the exploration of possibilities and therefore require high autonomy.

- **Tactical Teams** (e.g., military units, sports teams) that place prime importance on mission clarity. Here, the focus is on direction, clear roles and tasks, process, and accuracy.

No matter which type of team was studied, they found that the most successful ones shared certain characteristics. First, there was a clear and meaningful goal. The successful teams also had the right structure to fit the type of team, an atmosphere of collaboration, high standards, the proper external support and recognition, and effective leaders. Another of the key success factors was competent team members. They identified two types of competencies—technical (knowledge, skill, ability) and personal qualities, which tended to be determined by the type of team. The common features of competent team members were that they had to possess the essential skills and abilities, they had to have a strong desire to be on the team and contribute, and they had to have the ability to collaborate (or, in the terminology of Chapter Two, they needed strong *task* and *people* skills).

---

3   Larson and LaFasto (1989)

Psychologist and management team researcher Marie McIntyre[4] found five key success factors in management teams;

- **Strategic goals** (echoing the research and observations mentioned in Chapter One) are necessary for overall success.

- **Extensive networks** to facilitate the gathering of information and resources necessary for the team to make good decisions.

- **Collaborative relationships** (characterized by trust, respect, and successful conflict management) create positive perceptions among team members and facilitate success.

- **Effective information processing** is necessary for making good decisions when the team operates in a complex business environment.

- **Focused action**, which encompasses defining specific results, developing action plans, moving ahead in a timely fashion, including everyone in the planning process who should be there and following up to make sure plans are carried out is the fifth success factor.

Team Roles

Another seminal work on teams was conducted by English psychologist Meredith Belbin[5] over an extended time observing and training executive teams in the United Kingdom and Australia. He found that there were certain crucial team roles that showed up in the most successful teams. A team role was defined as a tendency to behave, contribute, and interrelate with others in a particular way. He identified eight such roles in his original research and demonstrated that a team with too many people playing the same role wouldn't perform as well as the more balanced teams. For instance, one of the roles was that of the clever, bright problem-solver. When he created teams with nothing but these people, instead of thriving, they never worked well together, and the teams comprised of people of only average talent and brainpower ate their lunch. He dubbed these Apollo Teams and observed that the Apollo Effect is a downside of having too many bright and clever people on a team—there is too much arguing about who is right, too much criticism of ideas, too much complexity, and too much intellectual arrogance.

Belbin clustered his team roles into three categories and gave them rather interesting names, some of which were not easily interpreted. In more recent versions, he has expanded the number of team roles from eight to nine and has renamed some of them for greater ease of understanding. The most successful teams are

---

4   McIntyre (1998)
5   Belbin (1981)

balanced, with no one role being overrepresented. And people often play more than one role on the same team.

- **Action roles** (Shaper, Implementer, and Completer-Finisher)
- **People roles** (Coordinator, Team Worker, and Resource Investigator)
- **Cerebral roles** (Plant, Monitor-Evaluator, and Specialist)

When working on teams, it is helpful to know our own most natural team role to understand how we may best contribute to the success of the endeavor. This model is an effective way to begin that process.

Getting Feedback

Getting feedback from the boss is often difficult. Very few people are comfortable or really effective providing solid, actionable critique. Many performance reviews are perfunctory—just another irritating task to be crossed off the list—and too often a source of great anxiety on the part of the giver and receiver.

- One good way to set the stage for getting the sort of feedback that will help you improve (and help you make sure you're getting your boss's needs met) is to occasionally set up an informal session away from formal performance review time.

  o Get on the boss's calendar several days in advance. Tell him up front that your agenda is to get his ideas and suggestions about how you can improve and how you can make sure you're focusing on the right (his) priorities.

  o One frequent response to a conversation like this is for the boss to ask, "Well, how do *you* think you're doing?" Be sure you're prepared to say what you're working on and how you feel you're progressing.

  o But be sure to ask directly if the boss thinks you're on track. The main thing here is that you need to be sure you and your boss see your job in the same way. You need to know how your boss would define success in your job. Bosses and subordinates often see things very differently. This leads to much unnecessary angst and heartburn.

- As mentioned earlier, other potentially valuable sources of feedback are structured rating systems (upward feedback, 360 feedback, etc.).

  o But you should be asking the right kinds of questions all along, not waiting until formal 360 time rolls around to get the information you need to be successful.

- o   Questions such as, "What do you need from me to make your job easier?" and, "What should I be doing more or less of?" should help.

- o   You should be asking your subordinates these questions on a fairly regular basis, but you also need to be aware of the needs of your colleagues in lateral positions and, to whatever extent possible, find ways to help them be successful as well. As stated elsewhere, you need to be seen as a positive resource by as many people as possible to help increase your influence and impact in the organization.

In Times of Stress

It seems to most people that the modern organization is in a chronic state of stress and uncertainty. Reorganizations, downsizing, rumors of change, new competition, and mergers, to name a few, are major distractions that can sap the energy, motivation, and creativity of people over time. When your organization is in times of increased stress, consider the following suggestions.

- Keep working hard and stay focused. It's far too easy to direct your energy outwardly and to worry about all the bad things that might happen. This causes people to lose focus. Remember that your main job is still to make your boss look good and to continue to build trust and credibility. You won't do it by wasting time worrying about things beyond your control.

- Don't waste time moaning or getting paralyzed. Act. The passive approach sometimes has great appeal in uncertain times. We think that if we keep our heads down, we'll avoid problems and eventually everything will be OK. That's not likely. True, there are times when not attracting attention to oneself has some survival value, but in times of crisis, change, and ambiguity, the people who act are usually the ones who come out better on the other end.

- If you don't have clear goals and tasks, get them. Then take action. But just be sure you're working on the right things. You need to have clear, focused, and appropriate goals. Granted, it's hard enough to get them in normal times in many organizations. But if you don't have them, you could draw the wrong kind of attention to yourself by working on irrelevant tasks. Be sure your focus is on things to help make the current situation better and to move things in a positive direction.

- Be sure to let others know what you're working on. You don't have to brag or otherwise be inappropriate about it, but you need to find some ways to ensure that your good works don't go unnoticed. One way to do this is to enlist the aid and cooperation of others, so that you're in the forefront as a formal or informal leader of the process. Also, be sure you're letting the boss know what's going on. This can be done easily by periodic update sessions. Put yourself on her calendar with an agenda of, for example, "Just want to keep you updated and to make sure what I'm working on meshes with your priorities."

- Stay upbeat and positive. Everyone's anxious in times of uncertainty. It's our natural tendency to seek cues from those around us about how to interpret what's going on. If we see people frightened, fearful, and anxious, the social comparison phenomenon kicks in, and we also start to feel that way. Therefore, to the extent that you can overcome those natural feelings and display signs of positive emotion and confidence, you'll make others less anxious. And remember, one of the keys to increasing your influence with others is the ability to make them feel good. Make it a point to smile. Greet others with interest and confidence. Don't show the fear you may feel. Practice looking confident.

- Stay in sight. The tendency to avoid the spotlight in unsettled times can lead to bad outcomes. It's easy to forget or ignore those who aren't around. If you're actively working on problems and obviously working hard to make the situation better, others will see you as adding value. If it comes to layoffs, who would you choose—the person who is on-site, working hard on the right things and trying to make others feel better, or the person who's not around? You need to be perceived as being helpful and as making a contribution.

- Remember, all other things being equal, toxic, negative people are fired first. Toxic people drain the energy from others. Nobody wants to be made to feel bad. Don't bring others down with idle negative speculation, gossip, or cynicism. Keep it to yourself.

- Keep expanding your skills and knowledge. People with more knowledge and skills that are useful to the company will last longer. Always take advantage of training opportunities. Even if things don't work out where you are, staying up to date and technically competent in your field makes you a more valuable potential new employee for someone else.

- Keep networking within the company. And within the industry. Outside contacts have obvious value if the outcome in your current environment isn't to your liking. Stay in touch with a wide array of people.

Summary

When you're in a new job, make a diligent effort to understand your new corporate culture and start off right.

- Be sure to find out from the boss what you're supposed to do and by when. Don't assume anything and don't rely on your interpretation of minimal cues or job descriptions.

- Introduce yourself to everyone.

- Keep your opinions to yourself at first. Listen—don't tell or sell.

- Don't trash your old company or former colleagues.

- Act in a friendly manner. Be the first to say hi.

- Play nice, don't gossip, and stay positive.

- Don't get locked into one group too quickly.

- Role models and mentors can be very helpful but be sure you find the right ones. And don't depend on them for too long.

- Find out quickly who has the power in the organization.

- Find a problem that can be fixed quickly and jump on it. This will speed you on the way to being seen as a credible force in the organization.

- If you're in a leadership role, consider all of the above plus:

  o Set realistic expectations. Be sure you adjust expectations as you learn more about the situation. Don't overcommit.

  o Talking and listening to others more than reading will help you understand the situation. Don't isolate yourself with financial analyses and reports.

  o Quick fixes don't work. Don't try to come up with the one right answer.

  o Get a few easy early wins. Don't try to do too much at once.

  o Get a quick and accurate assessment of your new team and don't stay with marginal team members too long.

  o Don't get captured by the wrong people.

Office politics are a fact of life. These are some general rules of thumb for making sure they work for you, not against you.

- Know what you want and stay aware of opportunities to move your own interests forward but heed the usual caveats about not hurting others and not appearing to be self-serving while doing so.

- Assume everyone's trying to do his or her best with the tools and information at hand.
- The grapevine can be helpful but also dangerous. It's a great potential source of information, but it's often wrong.
- Never, ever, betray a confidence. Stay away from personal gossip. Focus on business gossip.
- Assume anything you say will get around the organization.
- Be generous with your expressions of appreciation but try not to come off as a flatterer. Reinforce positive performance or behavior you like by showing your sincere appreciation.
- Make sure your complimentary comments are directed at behavior in the work setting, not about personal characteristics.

We all have to work on teams at some point.

- Although there are other characteristics of effective teams, clear and inspiring goals are the primary key to success, no matter what type of team is being considered.
- There are certain well-defined team roles that people gravitate to, depending on their talents and personalities.
- The most effective teams are balanced in terms of the team roles represented.
- The most effective team members have a balance of hard and soft skills.

It's difficult to get good feedback from the boss, but you need to make the effort to do so.

- One useful technique is to set up an informal session away from formal performance review time.
- Structured rating systems such as 360s can be of value.
- Ask the right questions.
- What do you need from me to help you get your job done?
- What do you need less of?
- What do you need more of?

In stressful times:

- Keep working hard and stay focused.
- Act! Don't waste time moaning or getting paralyzed.

- If you don't have clear goals and tasks, get them.
- Be sure to let others know what you're working on.
- Stay upbeat and positive.
- Stay in sight.
- Toxic, negative people are fired first.
- Keep expanding your skills and knowledge.
- Keep networking within the company—and within the industry.

CHAPTER 8

Conflict, Confrontation, and Difficult Interactions

Conflict is natural and unavoidable in human interaction. Most of us don't like it and try to avoid it. But it's always there, and we'd better learn how to deal with it. It's often suppressed in executive and other problem-solving teams, because people see it as threatening and unproductive, especially people who tend to operate mostly in the left side of the People/Task template described in Chapter 2. Conflict can be unpleasant. But it also can be a positive force for growth and creative solutions if dealt with in the proper manner. It must be faced and understood, not minimized or ignored if you want to achieve truly collaborative and productive outcomes.

There are two basic types of conflict—unnecessary/unhealthy and realistic:

- Unnecessary conflict stems from ignorance, error, tradition, prejudice, poor organizational structure, and other similar problems. For example, a conflict over turf in an organization characterized by silos is best understood as a systemic problem that can be remedied by the proper organizational incentives and possible restructuring, not as a potential source of creative solutions by a thorough exploration of opposing values and ideas. This sort of conflict is unnecessary and unhealthy, and should be avoided where possible.

- However, the other type of conflict, stemming from opposing goals, values, ideas, and interests is more realistic, healthy, and even necessary for continued organizational health. A conflict about the best way to tackle a new opportunity in the marketplace is healthy and desirable. In such situations, we need as much information as possible, and opposing views, even those we may feel are stubborn or idiosyncratic, are often helpful to contribute to a truly collaborative and creative solution.

There are two basic components of conflict—the substantive and the emotional. But there is also a deeper dimension, related to our identity. Productive conflict management requires dealing effectively with all three questions.

- Substantive—This involves the data and factual components of the conflict. The question here is, "What happened?"

- Emotional—There is often a strong emotional dimension to conflict—it's threatening to us. Never underestimate the power of emotions. The question here is, "How does this make me feel? How does it make the other feel?" You can't avoid dealing with emotions when navigating through difficult and conflict-laden situations because many times that's exactly what the situation is all about. Emotions must be acknowledged and dealt with, or they'll find a way to emerge again later, sometimes with more force and damage. As the authors of the book the book *Difficult Conversations* put it, "Have your feelings…or they'll have you!"[1]

- On a deeper level, conflict also raises questions about what this says about us, how it relates to our identity. If we perceive a threat to our identity, it can be quite disruptive and disorienting.

Handling Conflict

One way to increase your credibility in a team or other group is to be able to handle conflict effectively. Most of us are naturally inclined to see conflict as something negative, something to avoid if possible or to quickly squash if not. However, we need to realize that conflict is a natural part of organizational life and of life in general. And it can lead to better solutions and understandings if handled in the appropriate manner. A two-dimensional grid similar to the People/Task template introduced in Chapter 2 is employed by Thomas and Killman and by Rahim to define basic styles of handling conflict[2] and to help understand how we typically deal with it. The styles of handling conflict illustrated by these approaches can be interpreted as conscious choices about how we will handle a certain situation and/ or as natural dispositions related to personality characteristics. In these models, the two dimensions represent a concern for self (assertiveness) versus a concern for others (cooperativeness).

---

1   Stone, Patton, and Heen (1999)
2   Thomas and Killman (1974), Rahim (1983)

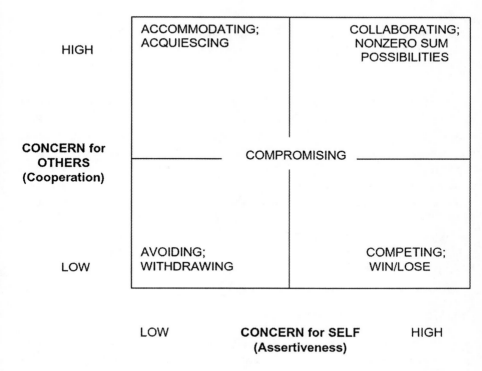

From interaction effects of the two dimensions, we again see five general areas on the grid. In this case, they represent ways to handle conflict.

- Accommodating (smoothing): low assertiveness (concern for self); high cooperativeness (concern for others). Disagreements are minimized so that harmony is maintained. One party gives in to the other.

- Competing (forcing): high assertiveness; low cooperativeness. Disagreements are seen as power struggles. Outcome depends on who has the most power.

- Avoiding (withdrawing): low assertiveness and cooperativeness. This is the neutrality position. Having no dog in the fight relieves the necessity of participating in the conflict.

- Compromising (sharing): average assertiveness and cooperativeness. The compromise position assumes limited resources and that the best solution is to divide them. In this position, everyone wins something, but everyone also loses something.

- Collaborating (integrative problem-solving): high assertiveness; high cooperativeness. The collaborative position enables us to assess several alternative points of view and to investigate interests, not operate from previously chosen positions. As with the People/Task template of Chapter 2, this position takes the most energy, and there are some fights that just aren't worth the effort, but it also sets the stage for creative, innovative win/win solutions.

There are times when each style is appropriate. Some problems will go away on their own and are best handled by ignoring them. If the conflict isn't that important, it's best to let the other win. If you have the necessary information to make the decision, the legitimate power to do so, and no time to hear all sides, make the decision yourself and mend fences later. However, if the problem affects everyone, if maintaining relationships is an issue, if the problem is important, and if acceptance of the final solution is necessary, the collaborative approach is required.[3] True collaboration means that people will have to suspend their own positions (at least temporarily) in favor of exploring wider interests that are involved. Although it takes extra effort to get there, this focus on interests rather than positions enables a group to come up with creative expand-the-pie solutions.

Assumptions and Consequences

Our reactions to others depend on their motives—or, more accurately, on how we *perceive* their motives. If someone does something to cause us anger or difficulty, we respond much differently if we think they meant it than we do if we think it was an accident. A good strategy for minimizing unnecessary conflict and pain is to assume innocence until you have enough information to suggest that the other's motives are more malevolent.

- If we perceive that the person acted from innocence (not realizing the impact of actions, not thinking, etc.), we're likely to react with understanding, humor, or compassion.

- If we feel the person was conscious of his actions and their impact, we react with heightened concern, anger, and disapproval.

- If we perceive that the person acted with hostility toward us, we're prone to react with even stronger anger, hostility, and resentment.

- The more we perceive the person's conscious and hostile intent, the more likely we are to get into the retaliatory cycle and have things spiral downhill. The best tactic is to assume innocence until we have better data. This avoids much pain and anxiety.

---

3   Vroom and Yetton (1973)

- The retaliatory cycle[4] can be demonstrated by use of the ABC model described in Chapter 6.

  o There is a triggering event (the activation). The other does or says something to precipitate the conflict.

  o We perceive a threat (the belief). Whether the trigger was intentional or innocent, what matters at this stage is our perception of his intent, our belief system. This is the cognitive component of the cycle.

  o We respond with anger, the natural emotional response to perceived threat and necessary mobilizing energy for self-protection (the consequences). This is the emotional component of the cycle that leads to actions.

    ▪ Our response to the anger could be noncommunication and withdrawal or direct retaliation. This is the action component of the cycle.

    ▪ The reaction is the natural and logical consequence of your response to the initial trigger. It can lead to a repetitive process or reverberating circuit, triggering negative responses in the other.

- From the earlier presentation of the ABC model, we saw that the way out of the negative spiral is to change our thinking. Cognition affects emotion. Emotion causes action. To avoid an unnecessary negative cycle, assume innocence!

Guidelines for Handling Conflict

- Forget trying to change the other person. It won't happen!

- Our natural tendency is to argue whenever there is conflict and we're forced into defending or explaining ourselves. We do this because our first response is to assume we're right and that the other person is the problem. What we don't usually remember is that they think we are the problem. Our natural defensiveness keeps us from understanding their story and context.

- We see the world differently, because we have different information and different insights. We interpret things differently, and we are influenced by our unique set of past experiences. Our interpretations will naturally reflect our own rational self-interest.

- In any difficult interaction or conflict, we need to understand the other's perception, her story. To get there, move from an attitude of certainty to one

---

4   Dana (2000)

of curiosity. Why did she do that? What, in her frame of reference, caused her to behave that way?

- Remember, our first assumptions are often wrong. We tend to assume intent from impact. Failure to separate intent from impact leads us into the cycle. To break the cycle, assume innocence.

- Seek to understand, not to blame. Blame is counterproductive, but if we can figure out how the situation came to be, what each party's contribution was, then we can understand and avoid unnecessary difficulties in the future. Try to get away from the problem-blame-solution mindset and get more into the problem-solution mindset (active collaborative problem-solving). Try to get a sense of teamwork in solving this issue that's keeping us from being productive.

- Discuss and agree upon up fair-fight rules. Knowing the structure and having a mutual agreement about how and when to escalate issues helps manage conflict and keeps it within less-threatening boundaries. An agreed-upon and well-understood process for mutual escalation is quite effective in managing conflict productively.

- Listen carefully. We're especially prone to misread the other during the emotional tension of conflict.

- Avoid criticizing the other person. Nobody will be at his best and willing to collaborate when the other party is blaming or finding fault with him. It perpetuates the cycle.

- Look for what you have in common. Try to find a common goal. Build your solutions on common interests.

- After the conflict: evaluate and assess. What can we learn from this?

Summary

Conflict can stem from unhealthy, unnecessary sources (ignorance, prejudice, faulty organizational structure, poor information, etc.) and from opposing goals, values, and ideas. The former is unhealthy, but the latter may lead to better solutions and understandings.

The basic components of conflict are the substance of the issue and the feelings involved. However, on a deeper level the conflict also raises questions about our identity—what it says about us as individuals at our very core. These are the reasons most people find conflict to be so threatening and anxiety producing.

On the two-dimensional grid described by Thomas and Killman (and similar to the People/Task template presented in Chapter 2), there are five basic ways to handle conflict:

- Accommodating (smoothing): low assertiveness; high cooperativeness
- Competing (forcing): high assertiveness; low cooperativeness
- Avoiding (withdrawing): low assertiveness; low cooperativeness
- Compromising (sharing): average assertiveness; average cooperativeness
- Collaborating (integrative problem-solving): high assertiveness (concern for self); high cooperativeness (concern for others)

We need to remain aware of our *assumptions* and their *consequences*:

- Our reactions to others depend on their motives. Or, more accurately, on what we perceive their motives to be.
- The more we perceive the person's conscious and hostile intent, the more likely we are to get into the retaliatory cycle and have things spiral downhill.
- The downhill spiral can be described using the ABC model from Chapter 6:
  - o There is an activating event—something happens to trigger the conflict.
  - o Our belief system about this event (whether realistic or not) triggers a reaction.
  - o If it's a negative interpretation, the consequence is that we respond with anger.
  - o But if we challenge our irrational beliefs by actively disputing them and replacing them with more realistic interpretations, we short-circuit the cycle and begin to experience new and more positive effects.

Guidelines for handling conflict:

- Don't try to change the other.
- Try not to argue or defend. You need to understand.
- Appreciate that the other has different information and insights.
- Keep an attitude of curiosity. Try to find out why the conflict exists.
- Our assumptions are often wrong.
- We need to separate intent from impact. Blame hinders the process.
- Set up fair-fight rules.
- Don't criticize.

- Look for what you have in common. Build on shared interests and common goals.
- After the fight, explore what you learned.

CLOSING SUGGESTIONS

We hope this will be more than just an academic exercise. Our goal is to provide you with the context and insights to help you influence others so that you have a better chance of reaching your potential in your organization and in your life. To provide a quick frame of reference for using this material, please consider the following observations, suggestions and thought questions when you're faced with the need to influence others on any particular issue.

- **Know your purpose.** What are you trying to accomplish? What is the long-term result you're looking for? What are the intermediate steps that will move the process forward? Can you visualize success very clearly and intensely?

- **Know your target audience.** Most decisions are emotional decisions. Much of the input for decisions comes through the emotional and subliminal channels. But smart, task-oriented groups also need facts and data to help them along when the rational brain is active. What is the group like? Are they internal or external? Technical? Emotional? Creative? Know your audience. Do your homework.

- **Use the Laws of Influence.** Which ones can you use and in what manner?
  - Credibility.
    - Do you have the necessary expertise? If not, can you enlist the aid of someone who does? Who can you use as a reference/source? Do others in authority agree with your position? Are the facts on your side?
    - Do you have the trust of the group? If not, how can you increase their comfort level? (If you can't do this, you need to seek other battles to fight.)
  - Liking. How does your audience feel about you? Do you appear similar to them? Do *you* like *them?* Where are the commonalities? How can you increase the chances that they'll like you and feel positively toward you?
  - Reciprocity. Do they owe you one for any reason? Can you ask them for a small favor of any sort? Can you do anything for them?

- o   Consistency. Can you get them to commit to something small? Will they agree to any part of your message? Have any of them agreed with you before? Can you show that they'll be inconsistent with previous actions, beliefs, or positions by not accepting your message?

- o   Social comparison. Can you show that others—especially in their peer groups, reference groups, or groups they look up to—accept your position?

- o   Scarcity. Can you show that your information is new, scarce, or limited? Are they likely to gain special advantage from using it or agreeing with you? What do they stand to *lose* by not agreeing with you or accepting your position?

- **Be sure of your message and its worth.** Do you really have a message that is appropriate and based in reality? Is it worth fighting for? Do you truly feel that it will help the company? Should you keep your powder dry and wait for another opportunity?

- **Use these principles appropriately and carefully.** Will the use of any of these principles cause you to seem manipulative? Can you use them in the right way? Remember, once you lose trust, you don't regain it. As with any tool, the laws of influence can be misused. Take care.

We know from observation and research that people can develop their skills of influence and can learn to have greater impact by paying attention to the principles we've presented in this manuscript. With effort and focus on the right things, you can realize more of your potential. But it's up to you. All the tools and attention in the world won't help if you're not willing to try new things and break out of your comfort zone. Like anything worthwhile, it takes a little work. But it's worth the effort.

Thanks and best wishes for further success.

APPENDIX

As an example of the effectiveness of psychological assessment in business, consider the following case. A client undertook a crash program to rebuild its sales force. Executives of the company wanted to make sure they were selecting and developing the right people to handle global accounts (large, complex international clients) in an increasingly competitive and ambiguous business environment. We worked with them to determine the foundation competencies necessary for a candidate to perform effectively in this exceptionally demanding role, then conducted psychological assessments on internal and external candidates to determine their goodness of fit with the success profile. Over 350 people were assessed in a period of ninety days. The first year's revenue figures revealed that there was a clear relationship between the psychologist's overall rating and performance on the job. The average performance of people who had been rated "marginal" from the pre-hire assessment was a little under $30 million, while the average performance of those in the "acceptable" category was about $40 million. If the client had chosen just one more person who performed at the average level of "acceptable" candidates rather than one who performed at the average level of the "marginal" candidates, the net revenue increase for the year would have been $10 million. If the client had hired just six people in the "acceptable" category (who turned out to be only average performers in that category) rather than the six people in the "not recommended" category, the total revenue increase would have been over $70 million.

Although there are many other data points to verify that psychological assessment is a valid tool for predicting performance in an organization, this example clearly demonstrates a high return on investment.

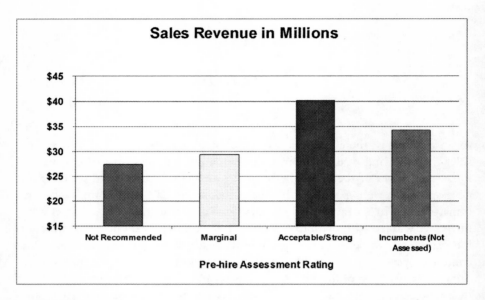

Psychological assessment is a proven tool for helping to select better people, but it is also useful in helping people to reach their potential. Each assessment provides not only information about the primary strengths of the person, but suggestions for further development as well. It is often the foundation document for developing a personal growth plan and for providing executive coaches and senior managers the information necessary to focus on developmental experiences that are likely to have the most payoff for the person and for the organization.

Clusters of Developmental Needs

Clients often ask us to review our assessments of their people for shared developmental themes to help them get the greatest return on their training and development efforts. The process of gathering such data involves not only a comparison of the average profiles of the personality inventory and cognitive test results of their people, but a content analysis of the developmental suggestions offered in the assessments. After analyzing several thousand assessments of successful senior executives and people in various fast-track leadership developmental programs, we clustered the most frequently mentioned suggestions for improvement into the dimensions listed below. (There are others that don't easily fit into any of these categories, but this list covers the large majority.)

1. **Influence and persuasion:** poor communication skills; needs to sell more effectively; may have self-presentation problems; introversion; possible bluntness; talks too much; talks too little; doesn't listen; oversells; unassertive; needs a more polished image; little boardroom presence.

2. **Interpersonal sensitivity:** too dominant, intense or impatient; too stubborn; may push people too hard; too competitive; needs greater general insight or political sensitivity; may be overly wary or suspicious, serious, or critical; insensitive or unsympathetic; ignores interpersonal or emotional issues; overly tough-minded; lacks insight.

3. **Organization and time management:** not enough detail-focus; disorganized; pay more attention to routine or maintenance aspects of the job; become more engaged; attend to administrative requirements; interests too wide; focus too broad; impulsive; skims over details; lets things slip through the cracks; misses things; doesn't use time efficiently; delegate more fully.

4. **Strategic thinking:** needs a broader viewpoint; get out of the details and trenches; see beyond facts and data; myopic; overly tactical; focus more clearly on long-range goals and effects; connect dots on horizon.

5. **Stress management:** overly emotional or volatile; lack of confidence; pessimistic; self-critical; relax more easily; tense/intense; anxious; internal conflict.

6. **Problem-solving:** low conceptual bandwidth; needs good second opinions; doesn't consider enough sources of data; slow or overly self-paced; better operating within range of experience; overly quick analyses and decisions; needs to be careful with new material.

7. **Overconfidence:** overly self-assured; needs to question self more quickly/thoroughly; play devil's advocate; don't assume you're always right.

8. **Rigidity:** overly structured; perfectionist; inflexible; overly procedure oriented.

9. **Workaholic tendencies:** needs realistic standards/expectations; can get out of balance; needs to back off and ease the pace; enjoy successes; catch your breath.

10. **Overly positive:** doesn't share bad news quickly enough; overly optimistic; doesn't consider potential problems/obstacles; puts too much of a positive spin on things; may ignore negative information too long.

11. **Team leadership:** needs to recognize/reinforce/motivate others; focus on team participation and development; build leadership skills.

12. **Too nice/agreeable:** overly accommodating; unassertive; tries too hard to please; values harmonious relationships over task accomplishment; can be taken advantage of; naïve; conflict-avoidant.

13. **Overly cautious**: needs to take more risks; drive things through the organization; too hesitant; may be threat-sensitive.

14. **Hard to read**: needs to be more open; could appear closed or political; needs greater awareness of impact; sends mixed signals; may be inconsistent.

15. **Financial acumen**: quantitative skills need improvement; needs finance for nonfinancial managers.

16. **Overly independent**: too autonomous; nonconforming; unconventional.

17. **Inexperience**: needs greater seasoning and experience; may not be fully mature.

18. **Downsides of intellect**: may inadvertently intimidate; too used to being right; loses interest too quickly with routine; interests too wide; boredom without significant intellectual challenge; overanalyzes; loses patience with slower colleagues.

Data from Executive Development Projects

The results of several analyses of the developmental needs of successful executives are presented below. The first one shows the graph of the clusters for a high-potential leadership program in a Fortune 50 company. All functional areas are represented by this group. It consisted of people who were roughly in the first third of their career trajectories.

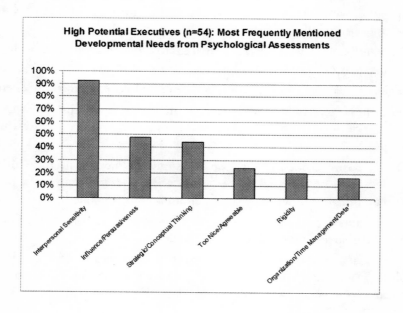

These are the results of the developmental needs analysis of a similar high-potential program in another company.

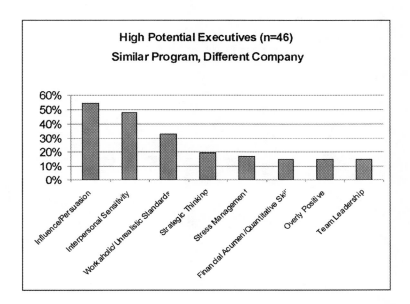

This is a sample of sixty hospital CEOs and COOs.

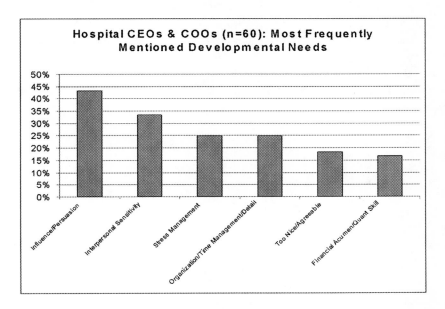

These are the results of an analysis of the officers and senior executives in a Fortune 25 company.

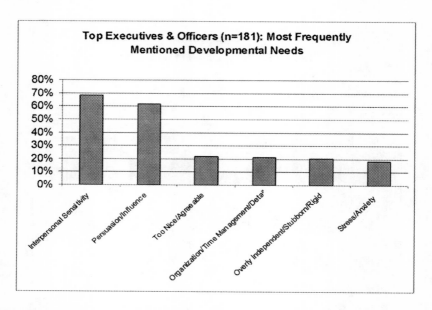

These are just a few of many studies that have shown the same trend. Most senior and high-potential executives need to further develop their insights regarding people and their skills of persuasion and influence. People in sales roles typically fare a little better, but a significant number of successful salespeople also have gaps in this area.

As you might expect, if these highly successful people on the fast track or in top executive jobs need to further develop their skills of influence, it's worse in the ranks.

REFERENCES

Asch, S. (1951). "Effects of Group Pressure Upon the Modification and Distortion of Judgment" in H. Guetzkow (ed.). *Groups, Leadership and Men*. Pittsburgh, PA: Carnegie Press.

Barrick, M. and Mount, M. (1991). "The Big Five Personality Dimensions and Job Performance: A Meta-Analysis." *Personnel Psychology*. 44, 1–26.

Bass, B. (1990). *Bass and Stogdill's Handbook of Leadership: Theory, Research, and Managerial Implications* (3rd Edition). NY: Free Press.

Belbin, M. (1981). *Management Teams: Why They Succeed or Fail*. NY: Wiley.

Blake, R. and Mouton, J. (1985). *The Managerial Grid III*. Houston: Gulf Publishing.

Blanchard, K. and Johnson, S. (1982). *The One Minute Manager*. NY: Morrow.

Cacioppo, J., Petty, R., Koa, C. and, Rodriguez, R. (1986). "Central and Peripheral Routes to Persuasion: An Individual Difference Perspective." *Journal of Personality and Social Psychology*, 51, 1032–1043.

Carnegie, D. (1981). *How to Win Friends and Influence People* (Revised Edition). NY: Pocket Books.

Caro, M. (1994). *The Body Language of Poker: Mike Caro's Book of Tells*. NY: Carol.

Cialdini, R. (1984). *Influence: The Psychology of Persuasion*. NY: Morrow.

Cialdini, R. and Goldstein, N. (2004). "Social Influence: Compliance and Conformity." *Annual Review of Psychology*, 55, 591–621.

Ciampa, D. and Watkins, M. (1999). *Right from the Start: Taking Charge in a New Leadership Role*. Boston: Harvard Business School Press.

Craig, K., Best, H., and Ward, L. (1975). "Social Modeling Influences on Psycho-Physical Judgments of Electrical Stimulation." *Journal of Abnormal Psychology*, 84, 366–373.

Dabbs, J. (1969). "Similarity of Gestures and Interpersonal Influence." Paper presented at the Seventy-seventh Annual Convention of the American Psychological Association, Washington, D.C.

Dana, D. (2000). *Conflict Resolution*. NY: McGraw-Hill.

Dion, K., Berscheid, E., and Walster, E. (1972). "What is Beautiful is Good." *Journal of Personality and Social Psychology*, 24, 285–290.

Ekman, P. (2003*). Emotions Revealed*. NY: Times Books.

Ellis, A. (1998). *A Guide to Rational Living* (Third Revision). NY: Wilshire.

Festinger, L. (1954). "A Theory of Social Comparison Processes." *Human Relations*, 7, 117–40.

Festinger, L. (1957). *A Theory of Cognitive Dissonance*. Stanford, CA: Stanford University Press.

Freedman, J. and Fraser, S. (1966). "Compliance without Pressure: The Foot-in-the-Door Technique." *Journal of Personality and Social Psychology*, 4, 195–202.

Goffman, E. (1959). *The Presentation of Self in Everyday Life*. NY: Doubleday.

Goleman, D. (1995). *Emotional Intelligence: Why It Can Matter More than IQ*. NY: Bantam Books.

Haygood, M. and Golson, H. (2001). *eTest Online Assessment Services*. Atlanta: Management Psychology Group.

Jones, J. (2004). "How Do I Love Thee? Let Me Count the Js." *Journal of Personality and Social Psychology*, 87, 5.

Kaplan, R. and Kaiser, R. (2003). "Rethinking a Classic Distinction in Leadership: Implications for the Assessment and Development of Executives." *Consulting Psychology Journal: Practice and Research*, 55, 1, 15–25.

Laney, M. (2002). *The Introvert Advantage: How to Thrive in an Extravert World*. NY: Workman.

Larson, C. and LaFasto, F. (1989). *Teamwork: What Must Go Right/What Can Go Wrong*. Newbury Park, CA: Sage.

Latham, G. and Wexley, K. (1982). *Increasing Productivity through Performance Appraisal.* Reading, MA: Addison-Wesley.

Linver, S. (1994). *Speak and Get Results: The Complete Guide to Speeches and Presentations That Work in Any Business Situation.* NY: Fireside.

McIntyre, M. (1998). *The Management Team Handbook: Five Key Strategies for Maximizing Group Performance.* San Francisco: Jossey-Bass.

Miles, R. (1997). *Leading Corporate Transformation: A Blueprint for Business Renewal.* San Francisco: Jossey-Bass.

Milgram, S. (1974). *Obedience to Authority.* NY: Harper & Row.

Milgram, S., Bickman, L. and, Berkowitz, L. (1969). "Note on the Drawing Power of Crowds of Different Size." *Journal of Personality & Social Psychology*, 13(2), 79–82.

Molloy, J. (1988). *John T. Molloy's New Dress for Success.* NY: Warner Books.

Mowen, J. and Cialdini, R. (1980). "On Implementing the Door-in-the-Face Compliance Technique in a Business Context." *Journal of Marketing Research*, 17, 253–258.

Myers, I. and McCauley, M. (1985). *Manual: A Guide to the Development and Use of the Myers-Briggs Type Indicator.* Palo Alto, CA: Consulting Psychologists Press.

Pizer, M. and Hartel, C. (2005). "For Better or Worse: Organizational Culture and Emotions" in Hartel, C., Zerbe, W., and Ashkanasy, N. (eds.). *Emotions in Organizational Behavior.* Mahwah, NJ: Lawrence Erlbaum.

Rahim, M. (1983). "A Measure of the Styles of Handling Interpersonal Conflict." *Academy of Management Journal*, 26, 368–378.

Savitsky, K., Epley, N., and Gilovich, T. (2001). "Do Others Judge Us as Harshly as We Think? Overestimating the Impact of Our Failures, Shortcomings and Mishaps." *Journal of Personality and Social Psychology*, 81(1), 44–56.

Schulte, M., Ree, M., and Carretta, T. (2004). "Emotional Intelligence: Not Much More Than G and Personality." *Personality and Individual Differences*, 34, 1059–1068.

Seligman, M. (1998). *Learned Optimism: How to Change Your Mind and Your Life.* NY: Simon and Schuster.

Stone, D., Patton, B., and Heen, S. (1999). *Difficult Conversations: How to Discuss What Matters Most*. NY: Penguin.

Thomas, K. and Killman, H. (1974). *Thomas-Killman Conflict Mode Instrument*. NY: Xicom.

Thorndike, E. (1920). "Intelligence and Its Uses." *Harper's Magazine*, 140, 227–235.

Tufte, E. (1983). *The Visual Display of Quantitative Information*. Cheshire, CT: Graphics Press.

Van Rooy, D. and Viswesvaran, C. (2004). "Emotional Intelligence: A Meta-Analytic Investigation of Predictive Validity and Nomological Net." *Journal of Vocational Behavior*, 65, 71–95.

Vroom, V. and Yetton, P. (1973). *Leadership and Decision-Making*. Pittsburg: University of Pittsburg Press.

Walster, E. (1065). "The Effect of Self-Esteem on Romantic Liking." *Journal of Experimental Social Psychology*, 1, 184–187.

Wilson, C. (1985). *Task Cycle Management*. Boulder, CO: Clark Wilson Publishing.

Zimbardo, P. and Ebbesen, E. (1970). *Influencing Attitudes and Changing Behavior*. Reading, MA: Addison-Wesley.

INDEX

ABC model, 67–68
    cognitive restructuring, 68
Authority
    credentials, 37
    image, 37–38
    law of, 36–38, 48–49

Competencies, types of, 1–2
Conflict
    components of, 83–84
    consequences, 86–87
    guidelines for, 87–88
    handling, 84–86
    retaliatory cycle, 86–87
    types of, 83
Credibility, 60
    and goals, 11
    I-competencies, 34–36
    keys to success, 11–19
    and law of authority, 36–38
    and law of liking, 40–44
    networking, 37
    and sales training, 63
    trust, 38–40
Cycle of results, 9–11

Door-in-the-face technique, 50, 58

Emotional Intelligence, 30–31
    components of, 31

Foot-in-the-door technique, 51, 61

Goals, 9–10, 64

Influence
    credibility, 34–36
    cycle of results, 9–11
    and emotional intelligence, 30–31
    law of authority, 36–38, 48–49
    law of consistency, 50–51
    law of liking, 40–44
    law of reciprocity, 49–50
    law of scarcity, 52
    law of social comparison, 53–54
    law of trust, 38–40
    motivation, 47–48
    obstacles, 24–27
    paths to, 48
    and personality, 27–31
    quick guide, 91–92
Integrity competency, 35–36
    trust, 35
Intellectual competency, 34–35
Intensity competency, motivation, 36
Interpersonal competency
    communication, 35
    influence, 35

Keys to success
    behavior versus attitude, 18
    influence, 18–19
    people management, 12–13
    self-management, 19–20
    task management, 12

Law of authority, 36–38, 48–49
Law of consistency, 50–51
Law of liking, 40–44
    keys to, 41–44
    socializing, 40
Law of reciprocity, 49–50, 61
Law of scarcity, 52
Law of social comparison, 53–54
Law of trust, 38–40
Leadership
    common deficiencies, 22–24
    credibility, 24
    influence, 24
    politics, 24
    trust, 24
    visibility, 24
Listening, 64

Motivation, goals of, 47–48

Optimism
    ABC model, 67–68
    explanatory styles, 67
    positive psychology, 66
Organizations
    culture of, 70–71
    feedback, 77–78
    stress, 78–79
    teams, 75–76
    transitions, 71–75

People management, 12–13
    cycle of results, 13
    influence, 13
    skills, 13
    and task management, 13–19
Personality
    and influence, 27–31
    introversion, 29–30
    extraversion, 29

Power, influence, 9
Presentations
    door-in-the-face technique, 58
    foot-in-the door technique, 61
    humor, 60
    and law of reciprocity, 61
    and law of scarcity, 57
    and law of social comparison, 58, 60
    and PowerPoint, 60
    preparation, 56–58
    primacy effect, 57, 60
    recency effect, 57, 60
    tips for, 58–61
Psychological assessment, 3

Sales training
    credibility, 63
    results of, 63–65
    trust, 63
Self-assessment, 4–7, 27–29
Self-management, 19–20
Stress, 78–79

Task management
    cycle of results, 12
    influence, 12
    and people management, 13–19
    skills, 12
Teams
    characteristics of, 75–76
    roles, 76–77
Trust, 4, 24, 35
    and credibility, 38–40
    establishing and maintaining, 39–40
    law of, 38–40
    and sales training, 63

Visualization, 64–65

978-0-595-38166-1
0-595-38166-9

Printed in the United States
88837LV00005B/202/A